TO FIND A JOB

Your 30-day action plan for success

Robin Casey

OLIVER
NELSON

THOMAS NELSON PUBLISHERS
Nashville

Published in Nashville, Tennessee, by Oliver-Nelson Books, a division of Thomas Nelson, Inc., Publishers, and distributed in Canada by Word Communications, Ltd., Richmond, British Columbia.

The Bible version used in this publication is THE NEW KING JAMES VERSION. Copyright © 1979, 1980, 1982, Thomas Nelson, Inc., Publishers.

Printed in the United States of America.

Library of Congress Cataloging-in-Publication Data

Casey, Robin, 1958–
   How to find a job / Robin Casey.
     p.   cm.
   ISBN 0-8407-9243-3
   1. Job hunting. I. Title.
HF5382.7.C37   1993
650.14—dc20   93-4503
                                         CIP

1 2 3 4 5 6 — 98 97 96 95 94 93

CONTENTS

INTRODUCTION

How to Find a Job will show you how to create your own personal strategy for finding a job. Studies show that most people entering the work force today will have to look for new employment an average of eight times during their career. After absorbing the information in this book, you will be well on your way to finding a job. Also, you will be equipped with the skills for finding a job in the future.

This book draws on the expertise of professional career/life-planning specialists and job-placement counselors to help people find satisfying jobs. Whether you are established in your field, changing careers, looking for your first job, or re-entering the workplace, the steps in the process are basically the same. Finding a job is not necessarily easy, but you can make it easier on yourself if you understand and follow the basic steps. Many people aren't hired because they don't know the steps or skip steps that seem elementary. However, practicing these steps and thoroughly completing each one will lead to your finding satisfying employment.

This book is designed to help you find a job as quickly as possible. In the next thirty days you can expect to create a thorough job search campaign. It may take longer to find an acceptable job, depending on the state of the economy in your area, whether you are trying to change careers, whether you currently have the skills and expertise necessary to successfully compete for the job you want, and whether your salary expectations are realistic.

The average length of time required to find satisfying employment varies, depending on the economy. In 1993 employment specialists estimate that the average length of time required to find satisfying positions for qualified applicants (above entry level) is six weeks to three months. In times of economic growth and expansion, the time required is much shorter. However, whether the economy is in recession or experiencing growth, the process for finding satisfying employment remains basically the same. Only the level of competition varies.

This book provides you with instruction, personal evaluation, action, encouragement, and food for thought. Adapt the instructions as they pertain to you. Each day you take the action steps given, you will be one step closer to finding a job. The Encouragement and Food for Thought sections will help you keep your spirits up as you work toward finding a job.

Finding a job is not your only reward. The process of seeking employment can be personally enriching. You may discover fresh new opportunities. You may meet people who become links to new career fields, members of your network, or new friends. In preparing to present yourself to prospective employers, you may rediscover abilities you lost sight of in your last job. I hope you can find the rewards along the way as well as a job that meets your needs and allows you to benefit your future employer.

---▲---

Seeking employment can be personally enriching.

In the best of times and the worst of times, people find jobs every day. You can be one of them.

DAY 1

Start with a Positive Attitude

Your attitude has great power. A positive attitude gives you confidence and enthusiasm. These attractive qualities can give you the edge over other applicants. Everybody loves a winner. Make an effort to perceive yourself as being on your way to finding a job, regardless of the obstacles, and people will be drawn to your side.

Following are things you can do to keep a positive attitude.

Take care of your health and appearance

Physical fitness will help you maintain good self-esteem. Eat a balanced diet. Dress up and groom yourself attractively every day. Exercise regularly with an activity you enjoy: join a gym, play tennis, take a dance class, run, swim, shoot hoops, join a bowling league or a baseball team. Take a brisk walk daily while you work at finding a job.

Vent negative emotions

Find a friend you can talk with openly. Express your feelings of anxiety, fear, self-doubt, shame, insecurity, hostility, rejection, and worry. Most people have these kinds of feelings when they are unemployed. These feelings are valid, but it does no good to let them dominate your life or your future. Vent them—and then let them go!

Spend time with positive people

The positive attitudes of others will help you maintain your own. If you aren't able to spend time with positive people, get some motivational tapes and listen to them.

Don't buy the excuses being offered

There are plenty of excuses offered for remaining unemployed: recession, quotas in hiring, layoffs, your age, sex, educational level, being underqualified, overqualified, and so on. These excuses won't help you, so stay away from them.

Take personal responsibility for your success

No one has the power to keep you from finding a job. Accept full responsibility for finding a job. Focus attention on what you can do to improve your current and future position. This kind of self-reliant attitude will make you more appealing to prospective employers.

▲

Focus on finding ways to improve your future.

Refuse to see yourself as unemployed

You may not receive a paycheck, but you don't have to be unemployed. You can work as a volunteer. You can employ yourself in the occupation of looking for a job. Let your next employer see how dedicated and thorough you are at marketing yourself. When he sees you excel over other applicants in the job-hunting process, you will have the advantage over your competitors.

Personal Evaluation

- What are you doing to take care of your health and appearance every day?
- In seeking to spend time with positive people, whom do you want to be near?
- How are you accepting personal responsibility for your future success?

Action

Write a plan of specific actions to help you maintain a positive attitude. Your plan might look something like this:

1. I will eat well-balanced meals, take a walk each morning, and play racquetball twice a week with

Sylvia (because she is the most positive person I know).
2. I will spend forty hours each week (or however many hours you are normally employed) at the job of finding a job.
3. I will borrow motivational tapes from the library and listen to them each morning as I walk.
4. I will look for humorous incidents to help me maintain my sense of humor.

Encouragement

You can change your attitude. Even if you are under great pressure to find a job, cultivating a positive attitude is the best approach to successfully presenting yourself.

Food for Thought

The winner sees an answer for every problem;
The loser sees a problem for every answer.
—Anonymous

Join a Support Network

Job-search networks are available to help you while you are seeking a job. A job-search support network is a group of people in the process of finding new employment. These groups allow you to meet others who are working at finding a job for moral support and to help one another. These groups are usually led by someone who is trained in career planning and placement, but much of the assistance comes from other job seekers like you.

These networking groups offer many advantages you would not have on your own. *Pooled information* is available. If one person discovers a job opening not suited to him, he will pass the information along to the group. The opening may suit another group member.

There is *mutual encouragement*. If you become discouraged, others in similar circumstances can help you
maintain a positive attitude. There is *shared knowledge* about the job-search process. Many of these
groups have forums on various facets of seeking a job,
during which those with specific skills can share their
skills and knowledge with others. For example, someone in the group who has writing skills may be willing
to help others compose letters or résumés. *An atmosphere of friendship* dispels the isolation that can un-
dermine a job search. Another plus is *the hope that
comes from seeing others find employment.*

---------------▲---------------

**Support networks offer
information, encouragement,
friendship, and hope.**

These groups can be found in most communities at low
or no cost. Some networking groups are offered free of
charge through government agencies or colleges. Others
ask that you volunteer services to the organization to
compensate for what you receive. Community colleges
may offer job-search workshops for a small fee.

Here are some services that may be available to you
through a support network in your area:

1. Expert guidance in the job-search process. This
   may take the form of free seminars, brochures, a

job-search library, or the advice of someone trained in career planning and placement.

2. Offices that you can use to make calls, use word processors or typewriters to create your résumé, make copies, fax information to prospective employers, receive mail, and so on.

3. Networking groups where you meet others who are looking for a job. These groups allow you to debrief after interviews, compare notes with other job seekers, share leads, give and receive encouragement, gain experience practicing interviewing and other job-search skills, share ideas of possible job options, and so on.

4. Job leads. Many of these groups are sponsored by organizations which employers consult with listings of their current job openings. There may also be directories and computer files to help you locate specific job leads.

Personal Evaluation

• What benefits can you see from being part of a job-search networking group?

• What are your hesitations about becoming part of such a group?

• Are you willing to overcome your hesitations to enjoy the benefits such a group could provide?

Action

1. Check the government section of the white pages in your local telephone directory under U.S. Govern-

ment Department of Labor and state government employment development program (EDD).

2. Call all the agencies listed that are associated with employment. Ask for information regarding any job-search networking groups they sponsor.
3. Gather all the information you can find. Don't stop after finding one support group.
4. Call adult education programs, college career-planning services, and placement offices in your area.
5. Find an office or place away from home to search. Be businesslike.

Encouragement

Making these preliminary calls can be frustrating and intimidating. However, your persistence will pay off. Remember, even if the receptionist doesn't have the information you need, that doesn't mean the services don't exist. Keep seeking until you find a group that will help you for the duration of your job search. If one group isn't right for your needs, find or start another.

Food for Thought

Two are better than one,
Because they have a good reward for their labor.
For if they fall, one will lift up his companion.
But woe to him who is alone when he falls,
For he has no one to help him up.
                          —Ecclesiastes 4:9–10

DAY
3

Commit
Yourself to
a Strategic Plan

Strategy is the art of devising careful plans to achieve a specific goal. Having a strategy for your job search will help you in many ways. By following a plan, you will achieve your goal more quickly and come closer to finding a job that will satisfy your needs and desires. Also, if you face setbacks, your overall plan of action will act as a guide to help you identify and correct problems. Using a strategy will distinguish you from many others who apply for jobs in a hit-or-miss fashion. In an interview, the fact that you have approached your job search in an organized and logical manner will be evident to a prospective employer. He or she is more likely to have a favorable impression of how you will approach any job you are given.

▲

Devise a job-search strategy for quicker, more satisfying results.

Many people limit their job search to the newspaper classified ads. Since 80 percent of all jobs above entry level are never advertised in the newspaper, your job search should reach beyond this method. You need a plan to find unadvertised positions that represent good opportunities for you.

You will better your odds by using a different strategy. Following the strategy outlined in this book will bring success if you are willing to thoroughly complete the action plan for each day. Resist taking shortcuts and skipping the basic steps.

Think of your job search as a marketing campaign. Your goal is to find a market for your services, availability, and the benefits you can provide an employer. Once you find a suitable market, you must communicate the benefits you have to offer in such a way that a particular customer (i.e., employer) chooses to purchase your offer by hiring you. Your job-search marketing strategy includes three parts, each of which must be accomplished to lead to success in finding a suitable job. Here are the three areas where you will focus your attention:

- Clarifying what you have to offer (your services)
- Targeting your market (suitable prospective employers)
- Selling your services (persuading someone to hire you)

Following is an overview of the basic strategy you will follow in your campaign to market your services.

Know your "product"

You will identify the features you have to offer in terms of personal qualities, availability, experience, abilities, understanding, skills, and special knowledge. Then you will determine how these features can benefit a prospective employer.

Clarify your goals

You will identify what you are seeking from a job and plan to find a job that meets your needs and desires. You will do this by clarifying career/life goals, personal interests, financial needs, family considerations, and work-related priorities.

Identify and qualify prospective employers

You will target the specific industry, type of organization, and geographic location that seem most suitable. Within this target range you will identify the names of one hundred specific companies or organizations to consider. Then, using a process of elimination, you will find ten companies that fit your needs and show an interest in the benefits you can provide.

Research target companies

Once you have targeted five to ten good prospects for your services, you will find out what you need to know before presenting yourself as a job applicant. You will discover current needs and problems within the organization, determine who will be making the hiring decision and the values used to make the decision, acquire a thorough job description, and find out how the company relates to their competitors.

Prepare to sell your services

You will plan the best way to communicate what you can do for the organization and help the employer envision you as part of the team.

Conduct the interview process

You will prepare your presentation, learn to inspire a vision of performance, identify potential objections, and prepare to answer them satisfactorily. You will also follow up on each interview to get a definite response and review what you can learn from the encounter.

Accept a position

You will make realistic choices about accepting a job that satisfies your needs and those of your new employer.

Personal Evaluation

- If you are used to relying on the classified advertisements, are you willing to try an unfamiliar approach to the job search process?
- Are you willing to commit yourself to taking each step (without shortcuts) so you can give yourself the best chance to experience success?
- Are you willing to make a commitment in this regard?

Action

My Personal Commitment

I,_____, am serious about my desire to find a suitable job. I am willing to invest at least one hour each day, for each of the next thirty days (if I am still working) or the hours in my normal work week (usually forty hours per week) to focus on this journey.

I understand that in order to reach this goal, I must be willing to grow on a personal level, to exercise courage to look at myself honestly, and to endeavor to meet all challenges. I will do my best in all of these areas.

I will focus my attention on taking each step in its entirety, without taking shortcuts or bypassing the action called for each day.

I make this commitment to myself this _____ day of _____, 19_____.

_____

Signature

Encouragement

This journey holds great opportunities for your future fulfillment. Give yourself the best efforts you can put forth.

DAY
4

Assess Your
Valuable Qualities

Your goal is to present yourself to prospective employers as an asset to their organization. You need to understand not only the value of your skills, but also the valuable personal qualities you have as an individual. When an employer must choose among several applicants with similar skills, the deciding factor becomes the personal qualities each individual brings to the job along with his skills. Employers can teach someone how to do a particular job much more easily than they can instill valuable personal qualities in his character.

Many employers will accept a somewhat lower skill level if the personal qualities they value are present in the applicant. For example, you may be an excellent accountant, competing with several other accountants whose skills are up to par with yours. However, if you have been able to convey that you are impeccably honest and loyal to your employer, you will have the winning edge.

To convince someone else that you have valuable personal qualities, you must clearly see your positive qualities and understand the value these represent to an employer. Everyone has many good qualities. However, if you don't focus on the good in your character, your weaknesses may overshadow your strengths in your mind.

Personal Evaluation

This exercise will help you focus on your positive qualities. These qualities form a foundation for the quality of work you perform. Following is a list of positive qualities that enhance job performance.

Focus on your positive qualities.

---

1. Circle any qualities that you have to some degree. I am:

sincere	analytical	patient
curious	artistic	dynamic
respectful	idealistic	convincing
able to lead	easygoing	loyal

controlled	funny	thorough
resourceful	dependable	honest
productive	a good team	helpful
self-starter	player	enthusiastic
able to follow	friendly	decisive
cooperative	confident	creative
attentive	goal oriented	conscientious
tenacious	hands-on	outgoing
teachable	purposeful	sensible
serious	sensitive	quiet
philosophical	low-key	inspiring
realistic	calm	faithful
driven	consistent	adaptable
balanced	cheerful	competitive
demonstrative	orderly	daring
considerate	diplomatic	committed
thoughtful	balanced	persistent
tolerant	secure	detail
positive	sociable	oriented

2. List the top ten qualities you circled, those that come to you most naturally.

Action

For each quality listed:

1. State in a sentence the quality you have.
2. Cite an example from previous experience, showing how you used this quality on the job.
3. Note how this proved valuable to previous employers or others.
4. Draw a conclusion demonstrating how this quality can benefit your next employer.
   Here is an example:
   "(1) I am detail oriented. (2) When checking sup-

ply orders for the restaurant I previously worked for, our supply costs were over projections and cutting into company profits. No one could figure out what was causing the overruns. By examining all the figures, I noticed that the pricing sheet being used was inaccurate. We had inadvertently been paying slightly higher prices than our vendors were charging. The difference was small on individual orders, so no one noticed. However, over the course of time the cost was considerable. (3) My attention to detail and natural curiosity led me to discover the error and save the company money. (4) If you have me on the job, you won't have to worry about the small details. You can be sure that they will be noticed and taken care of so that the company will reach its goals."

Encouragement

You may find it difficult to identify your valuable personal qualities because they are so much a part of who you are. Don't give up until you can list ten. If you need help, ask a friend; others may see your positive qualities more readily than you do. If you have a hard time listing these right off the bat, don't worry. That may mean you are naturally humble—a valuable quality indeed!

Food for Thought

It's not the qualities you have. It's the qualities you recognize you have and use that will make the difference.

—Zig Ziglar

DAY
5

Interview
Yourself
Thoroughly

Professional job-placement counselors know that the foundation upon which every new job is built is a thorough interview. The information gained from a comprehensive interview becomes the basis used to attract prospective employers. Since you are acting as your own placement counselor, you need to perform a thorough self-interview. The information you rediscover will form the basis for the steps to follow. So don't underestimate the value of giving this your full attention.

Your goal in conducting a self-interview is to unearth material you can use to persuade someone to hire you. The more you remember, the more can be adapted to demonstrate your value as an employee. Think in terms of the results you have achieved, not just a list of duties you performed. Look for examples from every phase of life highlighting the quality of your performance or how well you used the opportunities given you.

Employers often make hiring decisions based on factors other than past employment. You can show a prospective employer the kind of worker you are by citing evidence of your accomplishments in childhood, extracurricular activities, volunteer work, clubs, hobbies, athletic awards, and so on.

Cite life experiences to convince employers to hire you.

Make sure that each example you choose demonstrates the kind of person you are, how you respond positively to life situations, and (most importantly) how these qualities can benefit the employer.

You will also be looking for examples of how well you relate to others within an authority structure. Many problems at work stem from individuals who do not know how to relate appropriately to those under and above them in the chain of command. Being able to highlight and demonstrate respect for authority by citing specific examples is a valuable asset.

Personal Evaluation

Answer the following questions in writing:

- What did you learn in your childhood home that prepared you to be a responsible, highly productive employee? (Financial management, time management, cooperation, honesty, punctuality, interdependence, cleanliness, orderliness, respect for others, and so on are valid answers.)
- What subjects have you studied (throughout life)? How might these benefit a prospective employer?
- What subjects did you excel in during grammar school, high school, and college? How can your confidence in these subjects help your employer?
- What do you do regularly to better yourself physically, intellectually, spiritually, socially, and financially?
- What sports or extracurricular activities have you been involved in? What skills and character traits did you gain from this involvement?
- What awards, honors, or contests have you won? What might these suggest about the kind of employee you would be?
- How do you relate to authority? What evidence can you offer of how well you comply with those above you and respect the dignity of those below you?
- What motivates you to work?

Action

1. Select a notebook to use for keeping all your job-search information.

2. List every job you have ever held, including unpaid positions (such as internships or volunteer work).

3. For each job, recall a typical workday and workweek. Visualize yourself arriving in the morning and going through the normal routine. This exercise will help you recall parts of your job you might otherwise forget. List all duties and responsibilities.

4. For each position, make a list of all the skills you used on the job: clerical, problem solving, language, artistic, mathematical, interpersonal, financial, time management, communications, persuasive, mechanical, logistical, computer, record keeping, and so on.

5. For each position, summarize how you used your skills and personal qualities to help the organization make a profit or accomplish its goal (if it was a nonprofit organization).

6. After summarizing how you helped each organization achieve its goals, identify at least two specific examples for each job to back up your claims.

Encouragement

If you are willing to take plenty of time and thoroughly dissect your past, you will find a wealth of material you can use to convince a prospective employer to hire you.

Food for Thought

A pinch of probability is worth a pound of perhaps.
—James Thurber

Create
Your Personal
Benefit Statement

The motto "Find a need and fill it" is a capsulized description of a successful job search. When selling your services you must learn to think in terms of the needs you can fill for a prospective employer. If you focus your attention primarily on what you need and want, you won't spark the interest of employers on the lookout for someone who can do what they need to have done. You can help every prospective employer you meet consider you as a possible candidate by developing a personal benefit statement.

I once saw proof of this principle on a TV talk show. The hostess had invited back previous guests to see what had happened in their lives since first being on her program. One man had been out of work for a long time and was still unemployed. The show's hostess gave the man a prime opportunity to present himself to eleven million viewers who were probably already rooting for him. She said, "Please tell us what you can do." He responded (after a long pause), "Well, I can do lots of things. I could do most anything if someone would give me the chance."

Needless to say, the job offers did not come pouring in. If you are not prepared to tell employers specifically what you can do for them, you can't expect them to have an interest in hiring you. Your personal benefit statement tells employers in simple terms what you can do for them and their organization.

Whenever you are trying to sell anything, you must become familiar with both the features and benefits of your offering. A feature is some fact about the item or service you represent. If you were selling a car, the features would include items such as power steering, power brakes, V-8 engine, leather interior, driver's side air bag, convertible top, custom paint, pinstriping, and so on. The features are the car's selling points. The benefits describe what these features mean to the owner. The benefits of this car might be: The car is easy to handle and fun to drive. Your family will be safe while driving. The leather interior, custom paint, and convertible top will make you the envy of all your friends.

After hearing a list of features, the person listening might say, "So what? Why should I care about these things?" After hearing a list of benefits, the person will understand how these features can meet needs and provide benefits he may (or may not) care about.

Your skills and abilities are the features you have to offer a prospective employer. Learn to see your features in terms of the benefits they can provide in a work setting. For example, in presenting your abilities you may say, "I type seventy words per minute without error. I have excellent spelling and grammar. I am proficient at using Word Perfect 5.1 and 5.0 software. I am skilled in composing business letters, reports, and sales brochures."

After hearing this list a prospective employer could still say, "So what? What does this mean to me?" A benefit statement based on this list of features might read: "If you have me in your office you will never have to worry about correspondence leaving my desk with an error. You will never be embarrassed to discover that important documents went out representing your firm in less than perfect order. The stacks of reports and letters waiting to be typed and processed will disappear quickly. This will give me extra time to help with special projects that build your business and increase sales." After reading or hearing a benefit statement like this, the prospective employer understands how your features could fill possible needs in her office.

Personal Evaluation

- What are all the things you can do in a job setting?
- What skills and abilities do you have?
- What special knowledge can you use on your job?
- In what areas are you naturally talented or gifted?
- What kinds of jobs do you have an aptitude to learn?

Action

1. Drawing from your answers to the questions above, list all your features as an employee. Write these down on the lefthand side of as many pages as necessary to complete your inventory of features. Leave three spaces between each feature on your list. If you are thorough, this should take several sheets of paper.

2. Draw a line down the center of each page used. On the righthand side, list at least one benefit each feature could provide for a prospective employer in a business setting. Remember, each benefit will answer the employer's question, "How will this feature meet my needs?"

3. Read over all the benefits you can provide a prospective employer and circle the five you consider most significant. Using these five benefits as a basis, write a paragraph telling a prospective employer what you could do for his business or organization if given the chance.

   Start your statement by saying, "If you have me in your office or organization..." Then list the benefits without elaborating on them yet.

4. Read and rehearse your benefit statement until you have it memorized.

5. Expect that prospective employers will want you to substantiate your claims. Suppose they ask you to prove how you could have a particular effect on their organization. Write a proof statement using your features as evidence that you can live up to the claims you make. An example based on our previous case would be: "You can be sure the stacks of

reports and letters waiting to be typed and processed will disappear quickly (benefit statement)
because I am proficient at using the word processor
and I type seventy words per minute without error" (proof statement).

6. Enlist the aid of a mentor to help you talk through
your skills and abilities. Ask for his or her input in
listing and developing possible career paths.

Encouragement

Creating a benefit statement will give you practice in
thinking about what the prospective employer needs.
Once you are well versed in presenting the benefits
you have to offer, your ability to sell your services and
your self-confidence will be greatly enhanced.

Food for Thought

What lies behind us and what lies before us are tiny
matters compared to what lies within us.

—Ralph Waldo Emerson

DAY

7

Get Your
Facts and Figures
Straight

Before you apply for any job, it is important to get
your facts and figures straight. Be prepared with a
fact sheet of complete and accurate information for the
questions asked on job applications. This will give you
an initial advantage that may be the first step to the
job you really want. One small error on an application
may screen you out before you have a chance to meet
with the employer.

There are many good reasons to compile complete
and accurate information to be used when filling out
job applications. A line neglected on an application
may make you appear careless or unmotivated. A mis-
spelled word or grammatical error may cost you the
job. An apparent contradiction in dates on your job

history may be taken for deliberate dishonesty. If you are equal in competition for a position and the person responsible for hiring is unable to track down your references, he may opt to hire the applicant who supplied telephone numbers for his references.

Here is the information you will need:

- A list of all previous employers, including complete company name, street and mailing address, city and state with zip code
- Current company telephone numbers, including area code
- If the company is out of business, the name, address, and current phone number of someone who can verify your employment
- Accurate dates of employment and title of position(s) held
- Brief description of duties performed in each position
- Correctly spelled names of previous supervisors

Personal Evaluation

- Where have you worked in both paid and volunteer positions?
- Which of these companies or organizations are out of business?
- When were you employed at each respective job? Did any of these jobs overlap in time?
- Who were the people in each organization acting as your supervisors? Which ones did you get along with best?
- What work did you do? What results did you produce?

Action

1. Call each organization where you were previously employed. Record the following information:
   - The correct spelling of the company name and street address and the current telephone number.
   - Which of your previous supervisors are still with them. Write down their current department, title, and extension.
   - The dates of your employment as recorded in their files. You may find that your dates and theirs don't coincide. If there is a discrepancy, figure out where the error is and correct it. You may be surprised to find that the company has made an error. If so, gather enough information to confirm your dates of employment, call back, and make sure your old personnel file is corrected.
2. Obtain the phone number of someone who worked with you in the event of a previous employer's having gone out of business. Call other firms in the industry to locate where management personnel went when the firm folded. Call telephone information, trying to locate such individuals. Keep searching until you have a name, address, and current telephone number for someone who can verify your employment.
3. Compile a detailed job history with specific starting and ending dates for each organization where you worked. You may not choose to include every one on your application, but you need to have a clear time line in your mind so you can answer any questions regarding your job history. Recall and write out why you left each position. Be discreet.

4. Once your information is complete, type all the information in chronological order.

An important note

Although your primary intent is to gather information, make sure you present yourself as a viable job candidate to each person with whom you speak. Each person may be a link to a potential job. Remember, you have changed and the company has changed since you worked there. An opening may exist in your former company that might be suitable now. Also, every person you speak to knows others in similar organizations who may have job openings. This is a great opportunity to practice giving your benefit statement as a potential employee without undue stress.

Encouragement

Your time invested in correctly gathering this information will help you every time you fill out a job application. Also, the process may produce leads you never would have found otherwise.

DAY 8

_____

_____

Reexamine
Your Career/Life
Goals

Before moving on to present your services on the job
market, you need to reexamine what you want and
need from a job. The employer will not be overly
concerned about these issues. Therefore, you must
have the forethought to clearly identify what is important to you. This keeps you from wasting your time
pursuing jobs which will not meet your needs.

Knowing your career/life goals puts you at an advantage over other applicants. Once you know what's
important to you, you can research whether the company in question can meet your needs. In this way you
can prequalify the company in terms of the benefits
they have available for you. This allows you to be
wholehearted about your interest in a particular job if

it helps you reach your career/life goals. (However, in the interview your focus needs to be on explaining the benefits you can provide the company, not on what the company can do for you.) Following are some elements to consider.

Family life

Your current and future projections about your family situation will influence career plans. Consider how much time and energy you must devote to the needs of your family, the role you play and anticipate playing at home, the ages and needs of dependent children or elderly parents, your spouse's career plans, and any limitations these plans place on your flexibility. You may think of other factors that enter into this picture.

Financial needs and expectations

Your financial commitments and plans will directly affect your career plans. You need to know how much money you must contribute to your household in order to meet your budget, short-term and long-term financial growth plans, the importance of money in your priorities (as compared to such factors as status, being in a field you love, helping others, and so on), and what range of pay you expect and why.

Keep in mind that you will be paid according to the value of what you can do for a particular company. If you are firm on receiving a certain salary level, you must find an organization where your skills and education prove valuable. If you are changing fields or if technological changes make previous experience obsolete, you may need to accept a lesser salary or to sell yourself on the basis of using your skills in new ways that are valuable to your prospective employer.

Benefits

Most jobs or careers offer more than just monetary rewards. These fall under the broad category of benefits. You need to consider which benefits are essential, which are important, and which are relatively unimportant to your overall career/life goals. Also, consider which of these benefits are available to you through other sources. Consider the age and general health of family members and which benefits you must rely on over the coming years.

Time available and schedule preferences

Because of the changing needs and roles in our society, many companies offer flexibility in work schedules. Consider when you must be home to fulfill your role in the family, when you prefer to work, whether you want to work full-time or part-time, seasonally, days, nights, weekends, split shifts, swing shifts, and so on. Consider how much time you are willing to spend commuting or traveling on company business.

Location factors

The location factors to consider are your willingness to relocate, how far and how often you are willing to travel, how far you can realistically commute given the cost in time and money, whether the company allows for telecommuting (working from home while being connected to your office by phone and computer), whether you will be reimbursed for travel expenses, and so on. Also take into account the type of work environment, whether you will work alone or with others, the appearance and functional elements of the workspace, whether you will work indoors or outdoors, noise level, whether smoking is allowed, if the employees socialize, and so on.

▲

Your career goals should mesh
with your life goals.

Growth potential

Your career goals need to mesh with your life goals. Therefore, you need to have personal goals defining where you are headed in the next year, five years, ten years, and even twenty years. Knowing your long-term personal goals will help you answer a question of every prospective employer: How long will this person stay with our company? If you cannot convince the interviewer that your long-term goals for personal growth coincide with the growth potential within their company, you will probably not be hired. Therefore, know what you are looking for in terms of personal and professional growth and how you intend to grow within the company that hires you.

Personal satisfaction

Everyone needs some sort of personal satisfaction from their work. Consider how you derive personal satisfaction from your work, what motivates you to get up and give your best to your tasks every day, what you find interesting or stimulating about what you do, how you do it, the rewards you gain, and/or the results you achieve.

Personal Evaluation

- How does your family involvement affect your career goals?
- How much money must you contribute to your household budget?
- How do you plan to grow financially at a rate that keeps up with the growing needs of your family?
- How important is money in your priorities when choosing a job?
- What range of pay do you expect for your education, experience, and abilities? Why?
- What fields can use your education, experience, and abilities so that the organization can afford to pay you what you think you are worth?
- What benefits are essential or relatively unimportant?
- What are your time and scheduling preferences?
- What are your time and scheduling limitations?
- What location factors are you open to consider?
- What are your limitations regarding travel, relocation, and commuting?
- What are you looking for in terms of growth potential?
- What kind of work brings you personal satisfaction (primarily working with people, things, or ideas)?

Action

1. Write out specific personal goals for each of the following areas of your life: Physical, Family, Financial, Professional (Career), Community, Mental, Social, and Spiritual. Be sure to specify what you want, how much you want, the rewards you will receive from having reached these goals, and a time frame for achieving your goals.
2. Describe the factors included in a job that would meet your personal career/life goals. Include such items as type of work, salary level, benefits, type of schedule, type of work environment, location, and growth potential.
3. List in priority order these factors contributing to job satisfaction for you.
4. Put a star next to those items that are nonnegotiable. Circle those factors that you are willing to negotiate if the nonnegotiable items are in place.

Encouragement

Knowing what you want out of life will help you aim toward the type of job you can enjoy long term.

Food for Thought

Dreams and dedication are a powerful combination.
—William Longgood

Identify
What Is
Negotiable

When looking for a new job, you have an advantage if you do not limit yourself by assumptions that create unnecessary boundaries for you. A boundary is a line you have told yourself you will not cross in terms of what you will accept for a job. If your boundaries are too narrow, you may miss out on opportunities that could serve your needs very well.

▲

*The more flexible you can be,
the more job opportunities
you will have.*

The more flexible you can be regarding job boundaries, the greater range of opportunities you will have to consider.

You do need to have boundaries. There is no sense in interviewing for jobs that will not meet your financial needs or in which you would be unable to function successfully. The key is to establish your boundaries on the basis of your true needs rather than your preferences. You must know the following:

- A firm salary figure, below which you cannot afford to work
- A reasonable area within which you can commute
- The number of hours you have available for work
- When you can start
- Health factors that affect the kind of atmosphere in which you can work (for example, if you have asthma you would not be able to work in an office full of smoke without adequate ventilation)
- The kind of work you can and cannot do effectively

Beyond these factors, your other considerations are probably preferences rather than needs. Your preferences are important to keep in mind, but don't let them limit you initially in your job hunt.

Those who work professionally helping people find employment attest that people often find jobs they love in areas that originally were outside their boundaries. For example, one placement counselor worked closely with a manufacturing firm in a downtown location. This particular firm had great benefits and competitive salaries, was easily accessible by safe public transportation, and was operated by a fun and dynamic group of individuals. Repeatedly applicants would say: "I won't go downtown! I won't work in a manufacturing firm!"

However, time after time, the placement counselor persuaded suitable applicants to lay aside their preconceived notions to give themselves a great opportunity. Time and again, the applicants were surprised to find that the company was suitable. A number of these persons stayed happily with the firm for many years.

Personal Evaluation

- Consider the difference between your firm boundaries, based on real needs, and your preferences, based on wants.
- What are your firm boundaries?
- What did you previously consider nonnegotiable that you might now consider negotiable under favorable circumstances?

Action

1. Review the list of factors you said were nonnegotiable on day 6. Identify any you are willing to make negotiable.
2. List your firm boundaries.
3. List your revised preferences in order of priority.

Encouragement

By knowing where you need to draw the line and broadening your boundaries as much as possible, you give yourself the greatest advantage in finding a job.

Consider
All Your
Options

Before narrowing your focus toward specific opportunities, take some time to consider all your options. Career transitions give you the chance to make whatever changes you like. If you blindly race into a position similar to the one you just vacated, you may miss good opportunities. Or you may leave your next job because of a lack of personal satisfaction.

You have already clarified what you are looking for in a job and your boundaries in terms of what you are willing to accept. Now open your mind to fresh, unexplored options that may help you reach your personal goals.

Following are some options that may work for you. Consider each one in terms of whether it could be a positive step toward your career/life goals.

Going back to school full-time or part-time

Sometimes going back to school or supplementing your education can be a great career move. Financial aid may be available to help you productively use your time out of work and have some money to live on while you are a student. If additional education might help you in your long-term career plans, don't assume you can't afford time for education. Instead, make appointments to speak with representatives from suitable schools in your area. They can give you the facts you need to make this decision.

----------------▲----------------

Don't assume you can't afford time for education.

Also keep in mind that if you have an employment gap of more than one month, attending classes makes lapses more acceptable to employers. To have been studying is more acceptable than saying you simply could not find a job.

If you decide to go back to school, new job opportunities open up for you. Most campus career-planning and placement offices have listings of available jobs for students and internships. An internship can be a foot in the door to a great job offer if you perform well. An internship can also be a good transition into a new career field.

Military service

There are many jobs and career opportunities in the armed services. Consider visiting the office of your local recruiter to get up-to-date information on what each branch has to offer and how this option might fit with your career/life plans. Or talk to someone who is in the armed services to get a realistic picture of military life.

Self-employment

If your services are highly marketable or if you can produce a marketable product, you might consider self-employment rather than working for someone else. For example, you might purchase a franchise or other type of business. The information necessary to make this type of decision can be found in magazines related to entrepreneurial ventures, books in the business section of your local bookstore or library, through entrepreneurial organizations, or by speaking directly with franchise representatives from various companies. If you are considering self-employment, make sure your funding is sufficient to cover the cost of doing business and one year's salary.

Changing careers

If you have considered changing career fields, now is the time to entertain these thoughts fully. Speak to people in the field you wish to enter. Find out whether what you have to offer is of enough value to the employers in the field to warrant the salary level you need. If you change careers, you may need to take a cut in pay until your skill and experience grow to make your services worth more.

Personal Evaluation

- Could going back to school full- or part-time help you reach your career/life goals at this time?
- Have you considered career opportunities available in military service?
- Do you have marketable services and/or products that you could turn into a means of self-employment?
- Have you considered changing career fields? If so, what field would you like to explore? With whom could you speak about such a career change?
- What are the trade-offs you anticipate from changing careers? Can you afford the trade-offs?

Action

List any options of interest to you. Take action on any of the following suggestions that apply.

1. Call your local college or trade school and make an appointment to meet with a representative. Find out what financial aid is available, what classes suit your needs, and how long it would take for you to reach your career-related goal. Also, ask about student work programs or internships.
2. Call representatives from each branch of the armed services and make an appointment to get more information. Compare what each has to offer along with the level of commitment required. Don't make hasty decisions regarding military service, since all commitments are binding. Rather, take the information home and consider it objectively with input from family and friends.

3. Make appointments with people who currently run their own business in the field of interest to you. Ask whatever questions necessary to determine what it would take to start your own business. Get written materials that will help you make an informed decision. While speaking with those who are in business for themselves, remember to present yourself favorably. You may uncover a job opportunity along the way.

4. Set up appointments with at least three people who are working in the career field you are considering. Get their advice on the pros and cons in making such a change. Again, put your best foot forward. These discussions could turn into opportunities to work in their organization.

Encouragement

The crisis of being out of work could be a great opportunity to consider all your options. Don't pass up this opportunity.

Food for Thought

As important as your past is, it is not as important as the way you see your future.

—Tony Campolo

11

Tailor
Your Résumé

Your résumé is a written marketing tool. You can use it for a variety of purposes, but the aim is always to sell yourself to a prospective employer. A résumé can be an introduction, a guide for an interview's agenda, a written reminder of your best selling points to leave behind after an interview, or a customized persuasive tool to convince a particular employer that you understand and can meet the needs of her organization.

The word résumé comes from a French term meaning to summarize. Your résumé should be a short summary of your qualifications for a job. There are no hard-and-fast rules for résumé preparation (apart from the obvious requirements of honesty and accuracy). This gives you great freedom to choose how to use the résumé to your best advantage, depending on your work history and current career goals.

There are two basic types of résumés: the chronological type and the functional type. The chronological résumé is a brief description of your job history, including position, duties, and dates of employment, along with education, military service, and other training. This is typically organized in reverse chronological order, beginning with your most recent position and proceeding backward in time to show your career history.

------------▲------------

Your résumé is your foremost written marketing tool.

The functional résumé does not recount your career history. Rather, it focuses on what you do well—your areas of proficiency and expertise—then gives examples from previous experience to substantiate your claims. This résumé is organized according to various functions you perform well, such as management, sales, inventory control, clerical skills, accounting, and so on.

Use a chronological résumé if:

• You have a stable job history
• There are no gaps of more than one month between jobs

- You have held each job one year or longer
- You have grown steadily in status and level of responsibility within your field
- You are seeking a job in the same line of work
- You are seeking a job within the same industry

Use a functional résumé if:

- You are changing fields
- You are reentering the job market after an absence of more than three months
- You have held any of your jobs less than one year
- You have a pattern of moving from job to job
- You are looking for a different type of job than you have held before
- You are seeking the first real job of your career

There are many resources available to teach you how to write an excellent résumé. Visit your local library or college career-planning and placement office to find help in constructing your basic résumé.

The most important feature of a résumé is that it will work to your advantage. Following are some tips to help you get the results you want (progress toward receiving a job offer) from the use of a résumé.

Always be honest

Highlight your best points, but do not exaggerate or create experience you do not have. Many firms employ investigators to verify the honesty of claims made in résumés. Your personal integrity is one of the best qualities you can offer an employer.

Customize your résumé for each position you seek

Keep a chronological résumé and a fully developed functional résumé on hand. For each of these, include everything you have done and can do that might be of value to a prospective employer. (You should have gathered this information interviewing yourself on day 4.) Each time you research a job opening or a particular company and find an opportunity for an interview, find out as much as you possibly can about the company's needs. Starting from a list of the organization's needs, customize a functional résumé describing your abilities to fill the kinds of needs that company has. Highlight examples of success in previous positions that prove you could be an asset to the organization.

Additional tips include:

1. Never send your résumé ahead of you to the company if you can avoid it. Instead, ask if you can arrange an appointment and bring the résumé with you.
2. Never volunteer information on a résumé that could be used to screen you out. Such information includes age, marital status, number and ages of children, religious or political affiliations, dates you completed school, and so on.
3. Whenever you list job duties, be sure to include what you accomplished by doing your duties. Show how the company benefited from the duties you performed. Say, "I reduced supply costs from 14 percent to 5 percent of gross sales by skillful management and inventory control" instead of "I man-

aged kitchen staff, kept records of supply costs, running inventory."

Personal Evaluation

- Which type of résumé seems best suited to your needs?
- Are you willing to take the time and effort to prepare fully developed chronological and functional résumés?
- Are you willing to customize your résumé before interviewing with a particular company?

Action

1. Visit a library or career-planning and placement office to get several books on résumé writing.
2. Write complete functional and chronological résumés to draw from for your customized résumés.

Encouragement

Your résumé preparation will pay off by making your interviews more effective. A great customized résumé can help you need fewer interviews to get the job offer you want.

Food for Thought

You cannot make it as a wandering generality. You must become a meaningful specific.

—Zig Ziglar

DAY

12

Research Possible Job Sources

The first step in finding a job is to uncover as many job opportunities as you possibly can. Then you systematically focus on those in which you have the best potential for marketing your services. Your best markets will be those in need of the benefits and services you can provide, in an industry or organization having productive use for your special knowledge and skills.

The following list contains sources for finding companies, businesses, and organizations with possible job openings.

- Telephone directory (use listings of companies in your target area and preferred industries or services)
- Chamber of Commerce directory in your target area

- Friends and relatives (ask about jobs where they work)
- Teachers or professors (ask about companies they know of in preferred industry)
- Acquaintances (ask anyone you meet during your job search about jobs they may know of in your preferred industry)
- Your previous employer's competitors
- Database services for job referrals
- Classified ads in newspapers, business journals, and so on
- State employment service
- School placement offices
- Professional or trade journals (you can find names of trade journals servicing your targeted industry by checking the Standard Rate & Data Service Business Publications directory, which lists publications by specific business or industry)
- Professional directories (such as Dun & Bradstreet's various directories, Encyclopedia of Associations, Encyclopedia of Business Information Sources, F & S Indexes and F & S Index of Corporations and Industries, Fortune's Plant and Product Directory, Moody's Manuals, National Trade and Professional Associations, Occupational Outlook Handbook, Standard and Poor's Register of Corporations, Directors, and Executives, Thomas' Register of American Manufacturers, United States Government Manual, Who's Who directories, industry-specific directories, and the Directory of Directories to show you which directory has the information you desire)
- *Fortune Magazine*'s list of five hundred top companies
- New business listings in the newspaper or on file with

city government offices (new businesses may mean new jobs that have not yet been advertised)
- College or business school library or bulletin boards
- Business-related periodicals in your field of interest
- Job fairs

Use these sources to compile a list of companies to use as the beginning focus of your job search. You may or may not end up actually getting a job at one of these firms.

Personal Evaluation

- Are you willing to put in the time and effort required to compile a list of organizations that are possible job sources?
- Are you intimidated by doing research in the library, over the phone, and face to face with people you know?
- Are you willing to overcome whatever insecurities you have about this phase of the job-search process?

Action

1. Make a list of friends and relatives to contact for information on any organizations they know of that employ people in your area of expertise.
2. Create a one-minute summary of what you are able to do, what kind of organization you are interested in (finance, manufacturing, restaurant, and so on), and the kind of experience you have to offer. Practice this aloud until it feels natural. Whenever you talk to acquaintances, let them know you are

looking for new employment and give them your one-minute summary. Ask them to keep their ears open for companies that might be able to use someone with your capabilities.

3. Gather information from as many of the job sources as possible until you have a list of at least one hundred organizations to use as your starting point for your job search.

4. For each prospective employer get the company name, address, phone number, number of employees, and names of top officers.

Encouragement

Researching possible job sources is tedious work. By doing this work now, you will be able to distinguish yourself as someone who thoughtfully pursued organizations that could benefit from your services. This work will pay off later as you progress each step of the way toward your new job.

Food for Thought

If opportunity doesn't knock, build a door.
—Milton Berle

DAY
13

Go Prospecting by Phone

To get a job you must find or help create a need you can fill. The best way to discover needs is by prospecting—investigating many prospective employers to find those having immediate needs that you can fill. This process is much like prospecting for gold. With gold, you have to plow through a lot of dirt to find the valuable nuggets. In prospecting for needs you can fill, you have to make many contacts to unearth a few valuable possibilities for job interviews.

While prospecting, you are looking for an organization that has immediate needs you can fill. To discover these needs, never call and ask if there is a job opening. Rather, rely on your benefit statement and focus on finding out if the company could use someone who can provide specific benefits.

Here's how to approach a prospective employer. Call to speak to someone in the department where your research indicates you would most likely be of benefit to the company. Then say something to the effect of, "Could your company use someone who can balance a budget, cut supply costs, and increase sales?"

▲

Searching for a job is much like prospecting for gold.

If he has no potential openings or problems in those areas, he will say no. If there is a current need within the organization, he will ask you a question, such as "How much could supply costs be cut?" or "Why, are you an accountant?" If he asks a question, you can assume the need or problem is in whatever area he has asked about. He may not have a job opening per se, but may be thinking of replacing someone or be faced with a temporary problem that you could solve while demonstrating your abilities.

You then focus your attention on the area of interest he has indicated. You may choose to give a specific example of what you can do by citing how you cut supply costs by 50 percent in three months at your last position working for that company's competitor. Or you may ask more questions to find out about the specific needs and problems of concern. His goal will be to determine if you may be of help to him; your goal is to give enough information to whet his interest, but not so much as to rule you out of consideration.

Whenever you find that a prospect has a current interest, suggest that you are available to meet for further discussion. Never ask for specific salary or job descriptions. You may have discovered the opportunity before the details are clearly thought through. Once you convince the person you can be of help, you will be in a position to negotiate job description, salary, and benefits to make the job worthwhile for both parties.

Prospecting can expand your network.

Prospecting can also create networking opportunities. The person you reach may not have a need. However, she may know of someone in the industry who mentioned such a need or was complaining of having a problem you may be able to solve. By making her aware of what you can do, you create the opportunity for her to do a favor for a friend by pointing you in that direction. If she says, "Well, no, I don't have a need for those services, but my friend Joe at XYZ company might," ask her to call Joe and make an introduction.

Say something like, "I realize that you don't know me; however, would you consider calling Joe and letting him know that I may be able to help him?" If she is willing to make the call, thank her, get Joe's telephone number, and call Joe yourself in about thirty minutes. (Ask if she minds if you use her name when introducing yourself to Joe.) When you call Joe, begin with your original benefit statement.

Prospecting is a numbers game. You will probably have to make ten to twenty calls before finding a lead that results in an appointment or viable opportunity. Therefore, consider your calls as practice in polishing your communication skills and rehearsing your benefit statement without having to be in a face-to-face interview. Reward yourself for completing phone calls and collecting noes. Make it your goal to present your benefit statement twenty times to companies on your list and receive twenty regrets. This will help keep you from growing discouraged prematurely. Chances are good that you will find at least one valuable lead within each twenty completed calls. These will keep you motivated to go on through the one hundred companies you have on your list.

Whenever you find a lead concerning a need you may be able to fill, aim to set an appointment as soon as possible. Say something like, "I am available this afternoon or tomorrow morning. Would one of these times be convenient?" Give yourself enough time to do some preliminary research about the firm but not so much time that the other person loses interest.

Here are some tips to help you overcome any fear you may have of telephone prospecting:

1. Remember that a no is not a rejection of you. The person you reach doesn't know you. No simply means that the organization does not have the needs you are best able to fill.
2. If you are afraid to call someone in the department where you aspire to work, practice using your benefit statement with the receptionist. Receptionists are usually aware of the problems and needs within the company.
3. Put a mirror before you and smile at yourself while you talk. This actually does affect how cheerful you sound while on the phone and can help you lighten up if you are nervous.
4. Pretend to yourself that you are calling on behalf of someone else.
5. Remember, there is someone out there who truly needs the services you can provide. You are doing her a service by going through this process to find her need and let her know you are available.

Personal Evaluation

- What intimidates you about prospecting for job openings?
- What can you do to overcome your hesitations and give yourself the opportunity to discover great possibilities?
- Are you willing to complete twenty calls and give your benefit statement twenty times?

Action

1. Using your list of one hundred companies, make enough calls to give your benefit statement twenty times.

2. Keep prospecting with your calls until you have set up at least one meeting or interview in this manner.
3. Keep lists of all referrals and who made the referral. Send a thank-you note to each person offering a referral, and be sure to follow up all leads with a completed telephone call.
4. Go back later and work through all one hundred companies on your list.

Encouragement

You really can do this! It can even be fun if you make a game of it. The only difference between prospecting for job offers and a game is that in job seeking, the rewards are higher.

Food for Thought

The job hunting process may best be described as: NO
NO NO NO NO NO NO NO NO NO NO NO NO
NO NO NO NO NO NO NO NO NO NO NO NO
NO NO NO NO NO NO NO NO NO NO NO NO
NO NO NO NO NO NO NO NO NO NO NO NO
NO NO NO NO NO NO NO NO NO NO NO NO
NO NO NO NO NO NO NO NO NO NO NO NO
NO NO NO NO YES

—Tom Jackson

Create a Network
of Informational
Interviews

An informational interview is a dialogue in which you interview someone concerning your career development. This process offers many rewards, including the possibility of finding a back door into job openings you otherwise would never have known about. If you use this technique only as a means of finding "hidden" jobs, pretending to seek advice instead of being genuine, you will come across as manipulative. However, if you understand all the rewards available through creating a network of informational interviews, you will come across as sincere and reap all the benefits available.

In an informational interview you seek out people willing to answer questions about a given career field, company, or type of job. You begin the process by clarifying your career/life goals and targeting a specific industry or type of job you are interested in pursuing. Focus your attention on the differences between the work you are pursuing and your former job, the new benefits you are seeking that were not present in your previous position, the kinds of new challenges you long to tackle, and so on. Then turn to the questions you want to ask someone who is familiar with the type of job you are considering.

Setting up informational interviews

Following are tips for setting up an informational interview and getting referrals for further interviews beyond your current circle of contacts.

- Identify people you already know who understand the next phase of your career development. These can be friends, relatives, acquaintances, professors, and so on. Practice your first few informational interviews on these people with whom you already feel comfortable. Ask each of them if they know of anyone who could help you gather more information and if they would be willing to make a referral.
- Identify people in companies and organizations of interest to you whose accomplishments you respect or whose position is of interest to you. You can find their names and pertinent information about them by following the procedures used for researching an organization. Look for people who are already doing the kind of job you think you would like to pursue, people in your industry of interest who have been written up

in the press or professional journals (everyone enjoys being recognized for their accomplishments), and leaders in your area of interest who genuinely intrigue and inspire you.

• For the people you do not already know or do not have a personal referral for, it is most acceptable to send a letter preceding a telephone call to request an informational interview. (Do not send a résumé with this letter.) Here is the basic information to include in such a letter:

1. Address a specific person by name and correct title.
2. Introduce yourself and your interest in their field of knowledge.
3. Mention how you came to contact him or her in particular.
4. Politely request a brief meeting to ask some questions that would help you in your career development.
5. Cite a specific time you will call their office to try to schedule a meeting.
6. Close on a positive note of thanks.

• After sending out several letters to prospective contacts, follow up with the phone call at the appointed time. You should expect to schedule appointments with approximately half those you contact. If your call is met with regrets, be courteous. Take the opportunity to ask the person with whom you are speaking if there is anyone else in the organization or industry who might be willing to give you some information. Perhaps the particular person you targeted is too busy, but someone else may have time available. If not, pleasantly say thank you and wish the person a good day.

Conducting the informational interview

- Arrive at the appointed time, dressed properly to make a great impression. Greet the person with a firm handshake and a warm smile.
- Thank him or her for the time being offered. Then proceed to the purpose of your conversation.
- Start with a brief description of where you are in your career development, a condensed version of your experience, what you believe you have to offer an employer in this line of work, and what draws you to this particular career field. Then proceed to ask appropriate questions that draw upon the person's professional knowledge and expertise.
- Be prepared with specific questions. Here are some of the questions typically asked:
  1. How did you get to the position you now hold?
  2. What specific education, personality type, abilities, and skills are needed to excel in this career?
  3. Looking at my résumé (which you now offer to let the person view), do you see anything I need to do to supplement my experience and education before pursuing this career?
  4. Please describe a typical day and week.
  5. What is the future outlook for this industry?
  6. Where are the greatest needs, problems, and challenges in this career field?
  7. What is the best way to contact prospective employers or find jobs in this field?
  8. What is the normal salary range for this position for someone of my background?

- Be careful not to stay longer than the amount of time you requested. When the time is up, offer your contact the opportunity to conclude the interview. If he or she is willing to go on, express gratitude and continue until finished.
- Always ask for a referral. At the conclusion of your time together, say something like, "Thank you so much for this information. It will be very useful to me. Might you know of someone else in this field who would talk with me?" If she is willing, have her make a call of introduction. If not, ask permission to use her name in a letter of request.
- Offer the person your résumé in case she happens to think of anyone who might benefit from the services you can provide.

Following up after the informational interview

It is common courtesy to follow up an informational interview with a handwritten note of thanks. This is also a great way to leave a good impression and remind the person to pass your name on to anyone who might have a job opening.

Personal Evaluation

- Are you willing to create a network of informational interviews to help you pursue your next career move?
- Are you sincerely able to ask for and receive advice of this kind?
- With whom could you meet to practice informational interviews before approaching those you don't know personally?

Action

1. Compile a list of people you already know who would probably grant you informational interviews. Contact them and set appointments.
2. List at least twenty-five people you do not know personally who work in the field of interest to you.
3. Compose a basic letter to request informational interviews.
4. Adapt the letter to each person on your list and mail it.
5. Follow up with phone calls at the appointed time, and set as many appointments as possible. Obtain referrals and repeat the process as necessary.

Encouragement

Creating a network of informational interviews will speed up your job search and give you valuable contacts and information.

Food for Thought

There's nothing people like better than being asked an easy question. For some reason, we're flattered when a stranger asks us where Maple Street is in our hometown and we can tell him.

—Andy A. Rooney

DAY

15

Thoroughly Research Each Company

Having up-to-date information about prospective employers gives you the basis for your interviews and helps you determine which employers to pursue. The earlier you research each organization, the better you will be able to present yourself as someone who fits in with their people, values, and mission.

The information you are looking for

1. What is the mission of this organization?

    Most companies have a written mission statement, usually found in the employee handbook, public relations materials, or stockholder's reports. If there is not a written mission statement, find out what the company is trying to accomplish and formulate your understanding of the mission into a statement.

2. What is the history of the organization?

You will find the values of an organization by studying its history. You may also discover old wounds and goals that have yet to be realized. By knowing the history you can present yourself as moving in the same direction with the same values.

3. Who are the current officers?
4. Who will be doing the interviewing?
5. What kind of interview is typically conducted?
6. What is the company's standing in relation to competitors?

Every organization is either trying to reach the top of their profession or making sure they retain their position on top. Knowing the company's standing and why the competition is ahead or behind can help you perceive your opportunity to help the organization reach the top and stay there.

7. How is the company organized?
8. What is the company's reputation with suppliers, customers, and competitors?

Hearing accolades or complaints from customers, suppliers, and competitors will help you identify problems you can solve and needs you can fill.

9. What is the company's involvement in the community?

If you know the company sponsors a Little League team or has a float in the community parade, you can use these factors to establish common ground. You will also get a sense of the personality of the organization as expressed through community involvement or the lack thereof.

Possible sources of the information you seek

- Current and former employees

If you are considering a large company that serves the public, become a customer. Speak informally to those with whom you come in contact, asking about the company. If you find someone willing to talk, get as much information as you possibly can.

Former employees can be a good source of information. However, be careful to weigh the information given according to their personal feelings about the company. They may see the company in a negative light if they were fired, even if there was good reason for their release.

- Public relations department of the organization

You can call and request information without disclosing your purpose in doing so. Or you may prefer to let the public relations department know you are a prospective employee seeking information about the company. You may find a wealth of information, and the employer may be impressed that you took the trouble to find out.

- Published records and directories available at the public library or city hall

If time is short, ask the librarian to help you find as much information as possible about the organization. The librarian should be able to direct you to other sources for any information the library does not have.

- Trade publications, local newspapers, and magazines
- Any material published by officers or leaders in the organization (books, articles in trade journals, newspaper columns, and so on)

- Chamber of Commerce
- Better Business Bureau

Personal Evaluation

Are you willing to take the time and effort necessary to thoroughly research each organization before making a personal contact?

Action

1. Thoroughly research each company you plan to contact.
2. Compile the information you gather in a separate folder.
3. From the information gathered, formulate questions that display your knowledge of the organization.
4. Revise your presentation of what you have to offer in light of what you have discovered through your research.

Encouragement

The research you conduct before the interview will pay off in the interview.

Food for Thought

Dig the well before you are thirsty.
—Chinese proverb

DAY
16

Understand and Prepare to Meet the Employer's Needs

Every business or organization has a mission, even if there is not a formal mission statement. The organization exists to achieve certain results. The employer is looking for people who will help increase profits, reduce costs, serve their customers, and fulfill the mission of the organization. Employers and managers are continually thinking in terms of the bottom line, results, and/or profits.

To sell your services effectively you must learn to present yourself in terms of helping the employer accomplish the goals of the organization. Your first step is to determine the mission of each firm or organization you plan to approach for a job. You can do this in a number of ways. Check to see if the company has a public relations department. If so, ask for any information available that would include the organization's mission statement. If the company has no public relations department, ask the receptionist if a mission statement is available.

———————▲———————

Present yourself as someone who can help the company accomplish its mission.

Check the library for reference directories listing the company. A reference librarian can help direct you to the information you seek. Trade publications and industry magazines can also help you flesh out your skeletal understanding of the company's purpose. Don't stop your research until you can state clearly in one or two sentences what the organization is trying to accomplish by being in existence.

Once you understand the mission, consider how you can apply your "features" to help the company accomplish its mission. These translate into the benefits you have to offer this particular company. Consider where you might fit in the overall structure of the organization and how your work would contribute to its goals. Determine whether your services would help more in terms of sales, service, manufacturing, cost containment, or other specific areas. Suppose you see yourself in administration. This is not a full enough self-portrait in terms of understanding and meeting the employer's needs. You must think further until you can see how your specific administrative abilities would help the company become more profitable or productive.

Every organization has problems. You can be sure that the employer and managers are actively concerned about solving problems that threaten to keep them from achieving their mission. If you can identify a few key problems the employer is grappling with and show that you are part of the solution, you will have the rapt attention of that employer—and probably a job offer!

The first step toward identifying problems within an organization is to become familiar with the problems being experienced in the industry overall. There will be certain problems common for businesses of that type. Discover and understand these kinds of problems by reading the business section of the newspaper and trade journals or by talking to people who work in the industry.

You can approach this in two ways. You can target an employer, then try to find out the problems currently of concern to him. Or you can read up-to-date trade publications and newspapers with an eye open for problems that you might be able to solve. Then focus on the employers mentioned.

If you see a problem you can help solve, it is fairly easy to get an interview by calling the company and asking, "Would you be interested in meeting someone who might be able to help you solve this particular problem?" If you are correct about the problem being of immediate concern, you will likely get a prompt and enthusiastic invitation to meet to discuss the matter. This meeting can turn into a job offer when you prepare to show the employer how you can help him effectively accomplish the mission of the organization if he hires you to solve the current problem.

Personal Evaluation

- Are you willing to do the research necessary to know the mission of each organization before you seek an interview?
- Are you willing to change your focus from your own mission of finding a job to the mission and problems of the prospective employer?
- Are you willing to do the research necessary to identify the problems currently faced by your prospective employer?

Action

1. Choose one organization you want to consider for future employment.
2. Do whatever research is necessary, using the library, personal contacts, the company's public relations department, your telephone, and your imagination to discover the mission of the organization.
3. Write the mission statement in one or two sentences.
4. Write one paragraph stating what you can do to help the organization achieve its mission.
5. Do whatever research is necessary to discover three problems being experienced in this compa-

ny's industry. List these three industry-wide problems.

6. Write one paragraph for each problem, stating how you can help.
7. Do whatever research is necessary to discover one problem currently faced by the organization you have chosen.
8. Write one paragraph stating how you can help solve this problem and citing examples of previous successes that substantiate your belief that you can be part of the solution.
9. Contact the employer(s) and seek a meeting to discuss how you may be able to help the company solve specific problems.
10. Prepare an answer for the employer's question, "Why should I hire you for this position?" (Refer to day 24 for specific help.)

Encouragement

By understanding and preparing to meet the employer's needs, you make yourself considerably more interesting to the prospective employer. Take time to give yourself this advantage.

DAY
17

Visit
Three Agencies

You can use employment agencies in different ways to your advantage. You may find an employment agency that will help you find the kind of job you are looking for. If so, you have nothing to lose by allowing a professional job counselor to help you. On the other hand, many job seekers do not find a job by using an employment agency. Even if the latter is true for you, you can benefit in several ways from visiting such agencies. You can practice interviewing in a non-threatening environment, be tested to document your skill level, and get feedback regarding your professional image, communication skills, interviewing technique, and the appearance of your portfolio. Also, the employment counselor may give you leads on companies or industries you had not previously considered.

Following are some tips for using an employment agency.

1. If you can find an agency that specializes in your field of interest, choose this agency over one servicing a broad range of industries.
2. Never pay a fee. There are plenty of reputable agencies that receive their fee from the company doing the hiring. Visit these firms.
3. When calling initially, ask the receptionist which counselor has been with the firm the longest. Once you have this name, thank the receptionist and hang up. Call back later and request that counselor by name. Here is the reason: Your agency experience will only be as good as the counselor you are assigned. Turnover rates are high in employment agency work. Only those who succeed in placing applicants on a consistent basis stay for any length of time. Since agency work is usually a commissioned position, there typically will be some form of rotation for receiving applicants who phone or walk in. By finding the name of the most senior counselor, you ensure that you receive the best that agency has to offer.
4. Clearly state your limitations regarding the kind of job, salary, location, benefits, and work environment you are willing to accept. However, be careful not to limit yourself needlessly. You can always refuse any job offer you receive. You may be surprised that what you thought was a must may be-

come negotiable if the job offers other elements that meet your needs.

5. If you find a counselor you trust, who is willing to work for you, commit yourself to work with that person exclusively for three days. Counselors will not work wholeheartedly setting up interviews for you if they believe their efforts will be wasted because you are unavailable for interviews. If they have not found you a position in three days, continue to accept interviews set up for you by the agency, but let them know you are continuing your job search on your own as well.

6. Visit three agencies for a reality check. When you visit an agency, the counselor should tell you whether your expectations are in line with the job market and what you have to offer in your chosen field. If all three give you similar advice, reconsider whether your expectations are realistic.

7. Ask for and listen to the advice a good counselor has to offer. Placement counselors often are people who enjoy helping others. Even if the counselor is unable to place you, he may be able to offer good advice you can use to find your own position.

Personal Evaluation

• What hesitations do you have about visiting an employment agency?
• Are you willing to interview at three agencies for the practice and other advantages you may gain, even if you plan to find your job on your own?

Action

1. Look in the yellow pages of your telephone directory under Employment Agencies, or call your local Chamber of Commerce to get the names of three reputable agencies.
2. Call each agency, asking the receptionist for the name of their most senior counselor or someone who has been with the firm over one year. Thank the receptionist and hang up.
3. Call each agency back later, asking for the counselor by name to schedule an appointment.
4. Dress for these appointments as if you are interviewing for a highly desirable position. Take your portfolio with you, and practice your interviewing technique.

Encouragement

A visit to an employment agency may help you discover valuable human resources, both within yourself and in an employment counselor. Don't let prejudices keep you from obtaining any advantages.

Food for Thought

The great tragedy in America today is not the waste of our natural resources. The real tragedy is the waste of our human resources.

—Oliver Wendell Holmes

Prepare to Get
Great References

The kind of reference someone gives you can make the difference between receiving an offer and being passed over for a job you want. When a prospective employer gets great references about you, you gain a significant advantage over your competitors. However, if you proceed flawlessly through the job-search process and then receive a poor reference, you may lose your opportunity for a job offer. Therefore, it is important to make sure you get great references.

Your goal is to find someone from each organization where you were employed to give you a personal endorsement. You may not be able to find great references at every organization; however, you should be able to find one or two. If you supply the names and phone numbers of these individuals on your application, these positive endorsements, along with confirmation of dates and position titles from other companies, will leave you in good standing. Also, consider any teachers or professors who would be willing to endorse your character and abilities.

------------------▲------------------

A great personal reference can be your bridge to success.

Carefully select the persons you list as references. Choose those people in each organization who knew the extent of your job and appreciate the contribution you made. Possibly some of your previous supervisors did not appreciate your contributions out of a lack of attention or a negative attitude on their part. Don't list these people. List only those who knew and valued your work. Don't overlook great references just because these persons no longer work for the company. Find out where they work now and provide their new numbers on your application.

Don't be deceptive when presenting your best reference. If the application asks for immediate supervisor and the best reference you have was not your immediate supervisor, list the name of the reference you have chosen. But add a note to this effect: "Ms. Jones was office manager, not my immediate supervisor. However, she saw the direct positive effects of my efforts on a daily basis." If a previous supervisor would give a better reference than your most recent supervisor, list his name and add a note saying: "Mr. Roberts was my supervisor for three years and knows my work very well, even though he was not my most recent supervisor."

You must prepare these persons by contacting them ahead of time and being sure they are willing to serve as references. In some cases, someone who truly is enthusiastic about your job performance may be caught off-guard by a call from a prospective employer. If the call comes in the middle of a busy day or if the person stops to think up a reply when asked about your performance, his hesitation may be taken as a hesitation about you. If, on the other hand, you have called him in advance to prepare him for the calls, he will have a chance to think of specific positive things to say about you. You will also be able to verify that he holds you in high regard. If you find that some prospective references are not as enthusiastic as you hoped, you may want to select others who are more suitable.

When calling to prepare your references, remember that you may also be able to find leads for potential positions. Be courteous and tell each person with whom you speak what type of position you are looking for and what you have to offer a prospective company. In short, rehearse your personal benefit statement with each one. There are sometimes job openings at that person's company that may be unannounced or about to open up. By letting each person know you are available and what you have to offer, you may open doors you didn't know were there.

Personal Evaluation

- Who would act as a good reference for you from each organization where you were employed?
- Which of your supervisors acted as mentors and noticed your valuable qualities?
- Can you think of any teachers who would speak highly of your character and abilities?

Action

1. Call each person on your list whom you assume will give you a good reference. Let each know you are looking for employment and would like to list his or her name as a reference. Say something like: "I'm looking for a new job and would like to use you as a reference. Would you mind?" If the person hesitates, ask whether he has any reservations about the quality of the work you did for his organization. Then say, "Here are the dates of employment and job title I have on my records. Do these match the information you have?" If not, clarify until your dates and titles match his.

    Continue by saying, "I recall leaving that position because... Is this what you remember?" Chances are he may not recall why you left, and you can help refresh his memory. Then say, "In thinking back I would say I helped your company or department by . . . (then remind him of something good you accomplished while in this position). Can you remember any other positive contribution I may have overlooked?"

2. If he is not willing to give you a positive reference,

find out why. If he brings up previous mistakes or negative attitudes that make him unwilling to endorse you, try to minimize the negative effect this might have. Don't argue. Say something like: "You may be right about my previous performance. But I have changed my ways since then. I hope you wouldn't say anything that could jeopardize my chances at getting a job now, especially since I have learned those lessons the hard way. If you truly can't find anything good to say about me, I'd appreciate it if you would just verify dates of employment and my position."

3. If there is someone who would give you a great reference but is no longer with the company, find out where she is and call her to ask if she will endorse you. You may uncover openings at her new place of employment too.

4. Ask each great reference you find to tell you what he anticipates telling a prospective employer about your positive qualities and contributions on the job. Take notes as he speaks. Ask if he would mind having you write down what he just said about you for his signature, to use as a letter of reference. If he agrees, write a brief statement recounting the positive things he said about you. Send this to his office along with a note similar to the following example.

Dear Joe,

Thank you for the nice things you said about my job performance and your willingness to give me a good reference. Here is what I understood you to say about me. If this accurately reflects your opinion, would you please copy this on your company stationery (if appropriate) and verify the statement with your signature? I am sincerely grateful for your help.

5. Be sure to acknowledge each person's help with a thank-you note within a day or two.
6. Collect written letters of reference to take with you on job interviews. Keep them unfolded and clean so that they will help you make a great impression during interviews.
7. Type a list of references with the following information: name, current position and title, company name, daytime phone number with extension, and title each person held when they worked with you.

Encouragement

Making sure your references are in order will help prevent you from losing a job you may really want. Also, you have a reason to call companies to let them know you are available for hire. Most people feel some hesitation about asking for good references. You must overcome this hesitation in order to market yourself well.

Food for Thought

Let another man praise you,
and not your own mouth;
A stranger, and not your own lips.
—Proverbs 27:2

Prepare Your
Positive Image

In an image-conscious society like ours, preparing a positive image will help you considerably in finding a job. Any marketing campaign relies heavily on packaging to sell the product. The best of products will not sell if it is poorly packaged. The image you present is the packaging for what you are trying to market: yourself and the services you can provide an organization. Therefore, each element in creating a positive image will help you find a job.

Your goal in "packaging" yourself is to help the employer see you in the most positive light, in the context of what the company needs. You are looking for a job. The company is looking for someone to perform a job. Regardless of what kind of job you are seeking, there are certain socially acceptable norms that employers expect job applicants to follow. If you are willing to comply with the expected protocol, you will find your job much sooner. The best way to demonstrate your desire for a job is to act according to proper etiquette as you present yourself.

Dress appropriately

You may need to dress differently to interview for a job than you would to perform the job. If the job you seek requires casual attire, do not assume that you will get the job by dressing casually for your interview. Many people make this mistake. You will set yourself ahead of them by dressing for the interview rather than the job.

Acceptable dress for men is a suit and tie or dark slacks, a dress shirt, and tie. For a woman, appropriate dress is a business-like dress, skirt and blouse, or matched suit. Avoid low necklines or short hemlines.

Shoes should be appropriate to the outfit in color and style. Never wear tennis shoes or soft-soled shoes such as moccasins or athletic shoes. Women should wear stockings, even in hot weather. Simple pumps with low heels are preferred.

Keep accessories conservative and to a minimum. Avoid any accessory that draws more attention to itself than to you. Don't wear an accessory that may be a symbol of anything controversial (such as buttons with slogans, earrings for men, accessories associated with gang activity, and so on).

Follow personal grooming rules

Take a shower or bath immediately before each interview. Make sure fingernails are clean and well groomed. Your hair should be conservatively styled. Keep hair away from your face. If your hair is long, it's best to have it tied back in some attractive fashion. Men should shave immediately before interviews. Women should wear cosmetics conservatively to highlight facial features, without drawing attention to the cosmetics.

Demonstrate polite manners

Arrive early for your appointment. Thank the interviewer for the time and consideration he or she is giving you. Say please, thank you, excuse me, and other polite expressions whenever appropriate in the conversation. Follow every interview with a handwritten thank-you note as soon as you get home. (If you are in the running, the thank-you note may be an extra advantage to help the employer choose you over another applicant.)

Give a firm handshake

When you meet anyone in the business setting, extend your right hand, smile, and grip his hand with a firm handshake. If you are not confident shaking hands, practice until you are.

Use eye contact

If you don't look your interviewer in the eye, she may take that as a sign of dishonesty or insecurity. Just be sure to make eye contact occasionally.

Print your application neatly

Take your time and print legibly on your application. You will have the information compiled and spelled correctly on a sheet you carry with you. Be sure to copy the information accurately and spell correctly. Studies show that students who turn in neat work get higher marks than those whose work looks messy, even if the content quality is equal. The same holds true in making a good impression on a job application.

Present all material in a neat and orderly fashion

If you have written or printed material to show a prospective employer, make sure it is arranged in a neat and orderly fashion. Use a portfolio, briefcase, or other binder that will present the material attractively.

Observe telephone etiquette

When calling a company regarding a job, ask by name for the person with whom you would like to speak. You may want to ask the receptionist for the correct pronunciation or whether the person likes to be addressed as Mr., Ms., Mrs., or Miss. (Then address the person appropriately.) Always be kind and considerate to the receptionist or secretary. Be brief and to the point. You want to show that you are aware of the focus on getting work done rather than chatting on the phone.

Treat everyone you meet with respect

You never know whose influence will be decisive in a hiring situation. Be courteous and respectful to all employees with whom you come in contact.

Personal Evaluation

Are you willing to package yourself in a socially acceptable way to maximize your chances of finding employment as soon as possible?

Action

1. Using these guidelines, prepare your complete interviewing outfit. If you do not have appropriate clothes, borrow or purchase whatever you need to present yourself in a positive image.
2. If you have materials or letters of reference to take with you, get a folder, briefcase, or portfolio that will look good on your interview.

Encouragement

When you are prepared to give a positive image, you will have greater confidence in your job-search process. Do everything you can to present your best possible image for the interview.

Food for Thought

It is never too late to be what you might have been.
—George Eliot

Polish Your Communication Skills

Poor communication skills are often cited as a primary reason applicants are not hired. Therefore, it is worth the time and effort necessary to polish your communication skills in preparation for interacting with prospective employers.

Following are several tips you can put into practice immediately to help you make a good impression.

Know what you are trying to say

The basis for good communication is to know what you want to say before beginning to speak or write. Spend adequate time thinking through what you have to offer, anticipating questions you will probably be asked, and rehearsing your answers to these questions. You may find it helpful to write out what you want to say in essay form to make sure your thoughts are logical. Reading over your answers will help you see any flaws and correct them before you must communicate verbally.

Listen

Listening is one of the most important communication skills. In order to sell yourself, you must help the prospective employer build a bridge between what he needs and what you can do. The only way to know precisely what the employer needs is to listen carefully. This time is not wasted. An employer who senses that you clearly understand the needs of the job will be inclined to hire you over someone who spends all her time talking about herself.

Here are some ways to make sure you are listening well. Ask thoughtful questions, such as the specific goals that are to be achieved on the job. Listen; then check back to see if you heard and clearly understood the answer. You can say something like, "Let me be sure I understand you clearly. If I were to be hired, my goal would be..." Then you can follow up by relating specific examples that demonstrate how you know you can reach each goal. Another trick to good listening is to maintain eye contact and to be sure your body language shows that you are paying attention. Nodding, leaning slightly toward the speaker, and making comments such as "I see," "yes," "all right," and so on will tell the person that you understand him.

Always be polite

Show good manners in all your interactions. Address the person with the title he or she prefers, such as Mr., Mrs., Ms., or Miss. If you are not sure what title the person uses, discreetly ask someone. Never use his or her first name unless invited to do so.

Use proper English

Avoid using poor grammar, slang, or jargon.

Demonstrate respect and courtesy

Never curse, use off-color language, or tell jokes that have any sexual innuendos, racial overtones, or degrading insinuations.

Rehearse and get feedback

One problem with correcting poor communication skills is that your language (which may be acceptable at home) may not be suitable for a business setting. You might make mistakes you don't recognize. Rehearse your communication skills with someone who can give you feedback about appropriate language use in a business setting.

Personal Evaluation

• Are you confident that you practice good communication skills when speaking with and writing to prospective employers?
• Are you willing to thoroughly think through everything you want to say before you say it?
• Are you willing to rehearse your communication skills and get feedback that can help you spot mistakes and make improvements?

Action

1. Find someone who works in a business environment to rehearse an interview with you. Ask for the focus of attention to be on helping you identify any weaknesses in your communication style.
2. Practice asking questions, listening, and then giving feedback to make sure you understood what was being said.
3. Make corrections until you are satisfied that your communication skills will be an asset rather than a drawback.

Encouragement

Gaining confidence in your ability to communicate well will help you get the job you want and make your interviews less intimidating. Every hour spent polishing your communication skills is an investment in a better future.

Food for Thought

People judge you by the words you speak.
—Rush Limbaugh

Review
and Organize
All Materials

As you have moved through your job search, you have been gathering information and materials along the way. To make the best use of these materials, you need to review and organize them. The materials will fall into these categories: (1) information for your portfolio (to be shown to prospective employers and those who grant you informational interviews), (2) information for your personal use in the interview (taken with you but not shown to the employer), (3) information for your personal use at home.

Preparing your portfolio

Prepare a portfolio of materials that substantiate the claims you will be making to prospective employers. These will include a résumé (tailored to the particular job), letters of recommendation, letters of commendation, samples of your work, awards and honors appropriate to your work, and so on. Portfolios are particularly helpful if the person interviewing you tends to be more of a visual than an auditory learner. Seeing proof of your claims may stay with him or her much longer than just listening to your oral presentation.

Choose an attractive folder; leather is best. Enclose each item in a clear vinyl or plastic cover so that it is attractively displayed. Identify the purpose of each item included, and plan how you want to use each item in your presentation. Rehearse using the portfolio as a sales tool to show what you can do to benefit a prospective employer.

Compiling support material for your interview

Following is a list of support materials you will need.

1. A calendar. Record every appointment as soon as it is made, and check your calendar each evening to prepare for your appointments tomorrow. Be sure to use only one calendar. (If you use more than one, you may forget to transfer an important appointment.)
2. A notebook. Use your notebook to list the pertinent information about each interview or meeting, such as: company name, address, correct directions to the address, where to park when you arrive, name of interviewer, and phone number (in case of emergency). If you are answering an ad, you may

want to paste the ad itself in your notebook beside the other pertinent information. After your interview, note the names of each person who was a part of the interview process (to send thank-you notes later) and anything else you want to remember.

3. A sheet of basic information to be reported on the job application. This information, compiled on day 7, should be typed and enclosed in a vinyl or plastic cover to keep it legible. This sheet includes names, addresses, and phone numbers of previous employers, correct and verified dates of employment, names of previous supervisors and references, brief descriptions of duties for each position, and reasons for leaving.

Organizing support materials

Your support materials will include:

1. Information on each organization and prospective employer. Keep all of this information in a folder. On the outside of the folder note the names of the people you have spoken with, date and summary of the conversation, name of the person who referred you to the company, and a brief description of any meetings or interviews to date.

2. Business-quality stationery to be used for cover letters and letters requesting informational interviews.

3. Businesslike thank-you notes. Choose notes in a simple style, without pictures, that simply say thank you. Send these to everyone who helps you in your pursuit of a new job.

Personal Evaluation

- What do you need to purchase to get your materials in order?
- What materials do you need to organize for your job interviews?

Action

1. Purchase whatever you need to help you organize and prepare your materials so as to present yourself in the best light.
2. Review and organize all the information and materials you have gathered thus far.
3. Prepare your portfolio with care; then review it with someone who is supportive. Consider what materials you could add to make your visual presentation representative of your best strengths. Gather these additional materials to make your portfolio a professional sales tool.

Encouragement

Your willingness to carefully organize and present important materials will show off your organizational skills to each prospective employer.

22

Inspire
a Clear Vision
of Performance

The best way to create a desire to hire you is to inspire a clear vision of what you will do for the organization. This goes beyond convincing employers that you have the ability to do the job. You must find a way to show them the superior level of your performance.

You might think of this in terms of what a political candidate must do to win the hearts of voters. It is one thing for a candidate to build a case that he or she has the experience, knowledge, and ability to hold the office being sought. It is quite another thing to create an image in the minds of voters of how life would be better if that candidate were given the job. Creating a vision of your performance can often give you a winning edge.

A large church had been looking for a husband/wife team to develop a full range of youth programs for their congregation and community. Throughout the ten-year history of the church, the ministers and youth leaders had never been completely satisfied with the quality or breadth of programs for youth. They had interviewed and actually hired several people who were not able to meet their high standards.

The couple who eventually won the position did so by creating a vision of their future performance, as though it were already a reality. After assessing the needs and problems being faced by the leaders, the couple envisioned what the youth program would consist of if they were hired. They then created a brochure (like those the church produced to advertise other programs) detailing what the youth program (yet to be) offered. When they met with the leaders for an interview, they displayed the brochure and asked, "How would you like to present this brochure to your congregation and have the high-quality youth program it represents?"

The brochure demonstrated that the couple (1) understood the kind of program the leaders wanted, (2) knew how to create such a program that balanced the needs of many facets of the congregation, (3) could fit in with the high-quality presentation of programs offered by other ministries in the church. However, the brochure also served a more important purpose. It led those making the hiring decision to hope and believe that the applicants really could do what they promised. The interview then proceeded, with the applicants providing examples and convincing proofs to show the leaders that they could make this hiring decision with confidence.

It takes a great deal of forethought and hard work to inspire a clear vision of your performance for each prospective employer. However, it is worth the effort if you know that the job would be a good match for your career/life goals.

Personal Evaluation

- Can you see the value of going beyond merely telling the employer that you have the abilities to do the job?
- Are you willing to put in the extra work and forethought required to inspire a vision of your future performance for your prospective employers?

Action

1. Consider the one position you would most like to have. Clearly envision what you would do to benefit that company if given the chance.
2. Decide upon some effective way to create this clear image in the imagination of those hiring.
3. Invest whatever time, energy, and money it takes to create the vision of what you can do with the position you seek.

Encouragement

Being able to communicate this vision to the prospective employer is your best hope of landing the job.

DAY

23

Focus on Opportunities: One at a Time

Conducting a job-search campaign requires juggling a host of possibilities, giving each the highest regard. You must find a way to keep your spirits up despite disappointments. You must always present yourself in the best light, treat each encounter as if it is the key to finding the job you seek, and be prepared to reconstruct your presentation for each prospective employer.

This process is demanding, both on a professional and an emotional level. To maintain the quality of your presentation, you need to develop the ability to focus on each opportunity individually. Although you may have several good job prospects at any given moment, you must treat each one as if it were the only one.

Following are some tips to help you stay focused on each opportunity.

1. If you have a good response during an interview, you may mistakenly assume that you have the position—even though no offer has been made. During the period of waiting for an official offer, you may be tempted to slack off in your pursuit of other opportunities.

   Many factors will influence whether you receive a job offer, even if the interview ended on a promising note. Until you have received a firm offer of an agreeable salary and definite start date, continue treating each pending opportunity as though it were the only one.

Treat each job opportunity as the only one.

---

2. Don't conclude that failing to receive job offers from your interviews means that you are a failure as a person or that you are not a valuable employee.

   Every job search involves a series of noes before you receive the final yes. Plan to use every interview that does not result in a job offer as helpful practice and as a source of additional information you can use for your upcoming interviews. In a slow economy or during times of industrial transition, many highly valuable employees are out of work.

3. Don't let the repetitive nature of the process dull your presentation.

Your fifteenth interview is the first interview this prospective employer has had with you; and this may be the job for you. Treat each interview with the same care and preparation you gave your first interview.

4. Don't give the same presentation to each prospective employer.

Each employer is focused on the goals, needs, and problems of his organization. Your success depends on connecting what you can do to the particular interests of each prospective employer. Therefore, before each interview do the necessary research; revise your résumé accordingly; plan a creative way to inspire a vision of what you can do for this particular company; and focus specifically on helping this employer reach her goals, meet her needs, and solve her problems.

5. Don't isolate yourself, especially if you are getting depressed.

The faith and confidence you have in yourself will come across in your interaction with prospective employers. If you are isolating yourself or getting depressed, reconnect with those who can encourage you. Maintain involvement in a job-search support group; spend time with friends who have a positive image of you; request and rely on encouragement from those who are supportive of you.

Personal Evaluation

• Which of these tips points out an area where you might have difficulty during a prolonged job search?

- Are you willing to address each of these areas so that you can give each opportunity your best effort?

Action

1. Each time you discover a new job opportunity, write the name of the firm at the top of a piece of paper. During the job-search process, write what you did for each step taken in pursuing this particular job to the best of your ability.
2. Use two clipboards to keep these lists in one of two categories: a viable job possibility or a closed job possibility. The first clipboard is for opportunities that have not yet been pursued fully. That is, you have yet to complete all the steps in pursuing the job; and you have yet to receive a firm yes or no. (If no, why not?) The second clipboard holds the lists for each position after you have completed all the steps and you have received a definite conclusion— either a job offer you declined or one that was deemed not right for you at this time.

Encouragement

By treating each opportunity and each person with full consideration and respect, you create your best chance for success.

Practice
Your Presentation

Once you have progressed to interviewing for viable job openings, you must fully prepare to present yourself in a convincing manner, address the concerns of prospective employers, and convince them that:

- You take the job search seriously
- You can benefit their organization
- You have skills, special knowledge, and experience to offer that relate to the particular goals, needs, and problems of their organization
- Your personal qualities will be valuable to the organization
- You will fit in with the people already working in the organization

- You will be a problem solver, not a problem
- You are likable

Remember to practice making a good first impression. Wear your interviewing outfit when rehearsing interviewing (to notice anything distracting in dress or appearance). Practice introducing yourself to the receptionist with a smile and a friendly, confident manner. Practice your opening line, such as, "Hello, Mr. Prescott. Thank you so much for this opportunity to present myself as a candidate for this position." Smile, give a firm handshake, and make eye contact.

Because the job interview is pivotal to any future opportunities, you should rehearse your answers to basic interview questions until you have perfected them—complete with specific examples and illustrations of past performance backing up the claims you make about what your future employer can expect from you.

▲

Prepare, rehearse, and adapt your interview presentation.

Rehearse the interview with someone supportive, who is successful in business, posing as your interviewer. If possible, record your practice interview on audiotape or videotape. Review the tape and adapt your presentation until you are fully satisfied.

Here are the basic questions that will be asked in most job interviews (in one form or another), along with helps to prepare you to answer them effectively.

Why should I hire you for this position?

Your answer should have these three parts:

1. I understand this position is designed to accomplish...
2. I know I can accomplish this because I have these skills... (List your skills and substantiate how they relate to accomplishing the goals of the organization.)
3. I know I can succeed here because I have had previous successes that demonstrate my understanding of how to accomplish such goals and my ability to overcome similar obstacles. (Cite one specific example of previous success when you faced similar challenges.)

Tell me about yourself—your strengths and weaknesses.

Your answer should relate directly to your valuable personal qualities (highlighted on day 4), presented in a positive light. Tell the interviewer a few of your personal qualities. Cite how each one will be valuable to the organization. For example, if you are an extrovert you might say, "I am highly personable, optimistic, and enthusiastic. Therefore, you will find that I make our customers feel welcome and important. When faced with difficulties, I never shy away. Instead, I am the kind of person who sees every problem as a manageable challenge and actually enjoys solving it. My enthusiasm sometimes causes me to go overboard on completing projects. Occasionally this means that I become perfectionistic and work more than I probably need to in order to do the job right. I guess some people would see this as a weakness, but my previous employers never complained."

Acknowledge that everyone has weaknesses, but that you have no intention of letting anything stand in your way when it comes to fulfilling the commitment you make to your employer. (Once you make this commitment, be sure to fulfill the promise. If you have personal weaknesses or problems that might interfere with your work, seek the necessary help to keep from burdening your employer with the negative effects of your personal problems.)

What do you want to be doing five years from now?

Here the employer is trying to find out how much thought you have given to your career/life goals and whether your future considerations will work to the advantage of his firm. You should have a clear idea of how your personal goals mesh with the goals of the organization. Stress the ways your needs and family commitments tie you into staying with the organization. State your career goals in terms of being more productive in achieving the goals of this organization. Note that you realize being part of the organization's success will result in your personal success. If your family commitments motivate you to stay with a company long term, you may want to cite your personal goals as added motivation for staying and growing with this company.

How do I know you will stay with our organization?

If you have targeted your search toward a job you will enjoy that uses your skills, special knowledge, and personality, you should be able to cite these as natural reasons to stay in such a job.

Since employee turnover is very costly to the employer, you must be able to convince the interviewer that you have good reason to stay with the job long term. If you are taking a cut in salary or benefits, you must convince her that this job is not just a stopgap measure until you can find the kind of job you really want at a higher salary.

How did you get along with previous employers and co-workers?

The employer wants to make sure you are able to work well with others and will respond positively to the authority structure of the organization. Whatever your honest response, be sure that you don't gripe and complain about previous employers. Focus on the positive aspects of your relationships. If there were difficulties, focus on how you worked to get along with others under challenging circumstances.

Personal Evaluation

Here are some additional questions to consider when preparing for your interviews.

- What were your major achievements in previous jobs? (Mention at least one, not more than three.)
- Why have you chosen to make the job changes you have?
- What would you like to do if you could have the ideal job? (Hopefully, you will be able to say that this is an ideal job for you, or at least that there is no ideal job—only opportunities in which your abilities and time can be used productively. Then reiterate how your abilities will be productive in this position.)
- How would you improve our company? (If you have constructive input on how you think company goals could be achieved or problems solved, give specific ideas. Be careful not to belittle the attempts being made and programs already in place. You may unknowingly belittle the work or ideas of your interviewer.)
- What attracted you to our organization?
- How do your family commitments affect your work?
- How does your management philosophy mesh with ours? (Be sure to know something about each company's management philosophy, and be able to verbally communicate your own philosophy.)
- How would you solve the problems we are facing?
- How do you react to pressure on the job?
- When will you be available to start work? (Never offer to leave your current position without notice. If you are willing to abandon your present job, the prospective employer would rightly assume that you may someday do the same to her.)
- What do you consider your three greatest successes?
- What do you consider your three greatest failures?
- What job functions do you enjoy most/least?

Action

1. If you feel you need more detailed information on interviewing successfully, find a book on interviewing techniques and educate yourself fully on how to present yourself.
2. Rehearse a mock interview with a supportive friend who is successful in business. Have your friend ask the questions listed here, plus others related to your specific field. Have him give you honest feedback about any part of the interview in which you did not make a favorable impression. Record the interview on audiotape or videotape.
3. Listen to or watch the tape, and note any changes you need to make or answers you need to develop further.
4. Rehearse until you are fully confident in the interview situation.

Encouragement

Your preparation now will make all future interviews more comfortable and give you an advantage over your competitors who have not prepared sufficiently. The extra work you put in now will save you time in the long run; you will probably have to do fewer interviews if you are fully prepared for each one.

Food for Thought

Practice makes perfect.
—Proverb

Overcome
Objections
and Hesitations

Finding a job you are happy to accept always involves overcoming objections and hesitations. First, you must overcome any objections or hesitations about you that occur to the prospective employer. You will not get a job offer until this is accomplished. Once the job offer is made or obviously pending, you must also overcome the objections and hesitations you have about the position, without losing the offer by raising more hesitations on the part of the employer.

Standard hesitations

There are a few standard hesitations every interviewer will have at the beginning of the interview. They are: Is the applicant being honest? Can this person do the job I need to have done? Will this person stay with the company long term?

The best way to deal with these standard hesitations is to be honest in every aspect of your self-presentation. Don't hedge on questions or skirt issues that are truly difficult. However, you should have targeted jobs where the truth about you or your job history does not keep you from being effective. An exaggerated résumé or "too good to be true" application may cause the interviewer to doubt your integrity.

Be sure to target jobs that you are fully convinced you can do well. Listen to the interviewer as he tells you what needs to be done. Then do not conclude the interview without presenting evidence that you know what needs to be done, how it should be done, and how your attitude and ability equip you for this position.

Also, target jobs that you can plan to stay with long term. If you know why you are planning to stay long term, be sure to explain your motivation for longevity even if this is not asked directly.

Weaknesses in your package

You may have weaknesses in your package: job history, skills, knowledge, experience preferred by the employer, or schedule availability. For example, if you have a history of short-term jobs (under one year) or gaps between jobs when you were unemployed for more than one month, you must expect hesitation on the part of the interviewer and prepare to alleviate it. You must give reasonable explanations for this pattern and a credible explanation of what has changed to make this job more than just another stopgap measure.

Hesitations illegal to mention

Although it is illegal to discriminate on the basis of age, sex, religion, creed, or color, you need to be aware of possible hesitations about you that may never be mentioned for fear of legal repercussions. Consider what prejudices might be held silently against you, and do your best to dispel stereotypes that may work against you. For example, a young woman might emphasize that she has never been late for work or called away early for personal reasons and that her attendance is excellent. This would help dispel possible stereotypical hesitations that a young mother would be distracted from work by the needs and emergencies associated with caring for young children. If you are over fifty, you might stress your excellent health. Whether or not these prejudices are mentioned, they may be present in the minds of prospective employers. Do whatever is necessary to overcome even the unspoken objections without being obvious.

Transferring skills and abilities

If you are changing fields or seeking a job that uses your skills and abilities in new ways, you must prepare to clearly demonstrate how your previous achievements and abilities prove you can do the job in question. You can accomplish this by actually showing the interviewer a sample or demonstration of how you would do the job or by giving logical evidence that shows how your skills and abilities apply. If this is the only hesitation standing between you and a job you want, offer to work on a temporary basis for two weeks to demonstrate your ability on the job.

You cannot overcome an objection until you identify

it. You can identify some probable objections during your interview rehearsal. At other times you may sense that the interviewer has decided not to hire you for reasons that are not obvious to you. If you come to the end of the interview and the interviewer seems to have lost interest or is trying to tell you nicely that you will not be hired, it is in your best interest to bring unspoken objections out into the open. You have nothing to lose, and you can make tangible gains. You may overcome an objection by responding directly to it and turn the interview around. If not, you still can gain valuable insight about how to present yourself to other interviewers without being blocked by the same objection.

Here is some good advice if you are concluding an interview for a suitable job and you sense that you are out of the running. Say something like: "Can you tell me what it is that might cause you to hesitate about hiring me? Is it . . . (then list something specific that you realize might be a weakness) that I was only on my last job seven months?" Wait for an answer. You may hear honest objections. If the interviewer divulges the hesitations, respond to each one as best you can.

Personal Evaluation

- Are you being honest in your self-presentation?
- Are you targeting jobs you are able to do and plan to stay with long term? Why should the interviewer believe this?
- What are the weaknesses in your package?
- What are the prejudices that might create unspoken

objections about you in the minds of prospective employers? What can you do to overcome these misconceptions without addressing them directly?

- Are you willing to ask for reasons if it seems that you are not making a favorable impression during the interview?

Action

1. Make a written list of every possible hesitation or objection a prospective employer may have about you. Plan to overcome each of these in your interview presentation.
2. Rehearse dealing with hesitations, objections, and difficult questions about the weaknesses in your application package. Again, role-play this part of the interview with a friend. Tape the session; review the tape; and make necessary adjustments.

Encouragement

There is no perfect job candidate. Everyone who interviews for a new position must overcome objections and hesitations. By expecting and preparing for this in your presentation, you will be better able to get the job you want.

Food for Thought

The best defense is a good offense.
—Proverb

DAY
26

Follow Up
Each Interview
and Get Feedback

Your application process is not complete until you follow up on each interview and get conclusive feedback. Your follow-up always includes sending thank-you notes to each company representative with whom you spoke within one day of the interview. If the interviewer gave you a specific time frame within which you would hear the results of the interview, wait until the specified time has passed. Then, if you have not heard from the employer, follow up with a phone call. If no specific time frame was given for receiving feedback, call the employer after one week. The least you should pursue by way of feedback is a definite yes or no. If the answer is no, try to find out why you were not offered the position.

1. Send thank-you notes

   After each interview, send a brief thank-you note to the interviewer and anyone else who participated in the interview or spent time with you. Reiterate your interest in the position and your confidence that you could do a great job.

2. Wait the appointed time

   If the time frame for hearing interview results has passed, call the interviewer directly. Say something like: "Hello, this is Robin Casey. I interviewed with you last Thursday afternoon. You mentioned that you would be making a decision regarding the position by now. I would like to know if I am still being considered for the position."

3. Call to ascertain your status

   If no specific time frame was given or if you were simply told that you would be notified, call after one week. Ask to speak to the interviewer and say, "Hello, this is Robin Casey. I interviewed with you a week ago for the position of . . . Please tell me if I am still being considered for this position."

4. Ask why you were not hired

   If the job was offered to another candidate, follow up with the interviewer to find out why you did not get the position. Be careful not to act defensively or to put the interviewer on the defensive. Your goal is to find out the candid reasons that you didn't get the offer. If you can get the interviewer to honestly tell you what factors kept you from getting the job, you may be able to adjust your future presentations.

   If you treat the interviewer with respect and sincerely ask for informed feedback, you may be surprised to receive good advice. By asking the person for other possible referrals or other types of positions that you may do well in, you may actually cause her to think of another position in her company for which you would be suitable.

▲

Sometimes your best feedback comes from interviewers who didn't hire you.

There may be nothing that you need to change in the interview process. Sometimes several qualified candidates apply for a position, and all present themselves well. In these cases, there will be some individuals who did a great job in the interview but who are not offered the position. If the interviewer assures you that there was nothing you could have done better, accept that and go on.

Personal Evaluation

- Are you prepared to write and mail out thank-you notes immediately following each interview?
- Are you willing to follow up on each interview to get a definite yes or no—and if no, why not?
- Are you willing to open yourself up to constructive feedback from interviewers who could help you identify areas where you could improve your presentation or where you could direct your future efforts?

Action

1. Purchase businesslike thank-you notes.
2. For practice on getting feedback, call the three agency counselors who interviewed you (day 17) and ask them for feedback, as you plan to do with prospective employers after interviews with them.
3. In your notebook containing a list of all interviews, leave a place to note when thank-you cards were sent; when you plan to call for feedback; the yes or no. If the answer was no, list the reasons given as to why you were not offered the position.

Encouragement

Following up and asking for feedback can be intimidating. However, if you are willing to listen carefully, you may discover a new direction or problems you can solve. This will keep you from repeating mistakes that keep you from being hired.

Food for Thought

We should be careful to get out of an experience only the wisdom that is in it—and stop there; lest we be like the cat that sits down on a hot stove lid. She will never sit down on a hot stove lid again, and that is well; but also she will never sit down on a cold one any more.

—Mark Twain

Make Necessary
Adjustments
in Strategy

If you have faithfully followed each step thus far and are not meeting with success in your job search, you need to make adjustments in your strategy. Following are some actions you can take.

1. Review the clipboards holding your checklists for each step of the process regarding each position sought. Make sure you have not scrimped on any of the steps, especially the first steps that help set the direction of what jobs you will target.

2. Check to see if your expectations are too high for the real job market you face. Are you asking a higher salary than employers are willing to pay for someone of your experience, knowledge, skills, and

job history? Are your boundaries too limited in what you will do to earn a living? Are your boundaries too limited in where you will work or what kind of working conditions you require? You may be right in feeling that you deserve the things you expect in a job. However, if the market allows the employer to hire people who have comparable skills, knowledge, and experience without having to meet the expectations you have, she will probably hire those with less demanding expectations.

3. Reconsider the reasons given for why you are not being hired. What can you do to keep these reasons from barring you from employment? For example, if you have been trying to change fields but keep being edged out by those who have more experience, perhaps you need to aim for a job in your previous field (where your experience gives you an advantage) instead of continuing against the odds. Or perhaps you need to get additional skills or experience through an internship or apprenticeship position.

4. After one month, check back with organizations where you were a viable contender for a position that was offered to someone else. If you made a good impression, you may find that new opportunities have opened up, making the organization a viable possibility once more.

Personal Evaluation

- What steps might you have missed or not fully applied yourself to?
- Are you willing to adjust your aims or approach to

the job search to give yourself a better chance of getting a job?

- If you are not still involved with a job-search network or if you never were involved in such a group, are you willing to become involved now?

Action

1. Make a list of specific new actions you can take to find a job.
2. Call back all firms where you interviewed over one month ago to see if the interviewer remembers you and if the company may have any current suitable positions.
3. List the changes you will make in the type of position you are seeking, the salary you will accept, or other areas in which you are willing to be more flexible.

Encouragement

If you will identify where you may have missed a step or aimed in a direction that is out of reach at the moment, you can make corrections that will lead to finding a job.

Food for Thought

I have not failed 10,000 times. I have successfully found 10,000 ways that will not work.

—Thomas Edison,
after trying an experiment 10,000 times

DAY
28

Make Realistic
Choices
and Commitments

When you receive a job offer, you will be inclined to accept the position. You will feel excitement over being accepted and seen as worthwhile. You may fear not being offered any other position if you decline this one.

In spite of the emotional intensity surrounding a job offer, you must keep your head and make realistic choices and commitments at this time. Following are the elements you need to consider.

1. Whether the job meets your basic needs. Consider whether you can actually live on the salary, make it to work every day given the commute involved, and integrate the demands of the job with your other

life commitments. If the offer doesn't meet these basic needs, you must negotiate a better offer or decline the position. Otherwise, sooner or later you will find yourself interviewing again and trying to explain why you were only in the position a few months.

2. Whether the employer will use your abilities to create a satisfying career choice.

3. Whether the job and advancement opportunities available are compatible with your career/life goals. You may find that this new opportunity helps you adjust your career/life goals. This is fine. However, if the job works against the things you deeply value and aspire toward, be careful about accepting such a position.

4. Whether you can really fulfill the commitments you are about to make. Be sure the employer's expectations are clearly spelled out in terms of job description, hours, working conditions, and so on. Seriously consider whether you are able and willing to make the commitments being asked of you.

5. Any hesitations or objections you have regarding the job offer, the working conditions, or the company. If you like much of what the job seems to offer and would like to enthusiastically accept the position, diplomatically bring up any hesitations or questions you have about the position that you did not ask previously. Once a firm offer has been extended, these kinds of questions are acceptable and will not negate the offer if you ask with a willingness to be flexible regarding the needs of the company. Don't wait until you have started work to bring these issues up. Do so while negotiations are

still under way so you can make an informed decision about whether to accept the position as it is.

Personal Evaluation

Before accepting any job, ask yourself these questions:

- Can you live with the demands and financial remuneration of this job offer?
- Does this job bring you closer to or further from your career/life goals?
- Are you willing to adapt your career/life goals for the sake of this position?
- Do the demands of this job create conflict in your personal life or family commitments? If so, how can these be resolved so as not to interfere with performing your job to the expectation of your employer?
- What are the specific detailed commitments you are being asked to make? Are you able and willing to keep these commitments long term?
- What hesitations do you have regarding the position? Are you willing to bring these up with the employer for the sake of clarification?

Action

1. Whenever you are offered a job, it is advisable to tentatively accept the position and find out the specific salary and start date being offered. Then ask for an appointment to meet with the employer in a day or two to go over the details and make whatever negotiations are necessary.

2. Use the time after receiving an offer and before your meeting to consider (with the input of your family and trusted friends) whether you can make a commitment to the position.

3. If you are still being considered for other positions that hold your interest, call these employers. Inform the interviewer or decision maker that you have received a job offer and that you would like to know when he can give you a definite answer regarding employment. If he is noncommittal, don't allow hopes of this position to sour you on the actual offer you already have. Trust that if the decision maker is serious about offering you a position, he will not want to lose you and will let you know quickly. If you have not heard from him in twenty-four hours, dismiss the thought.

Encouragement

A good dose of realism always works to your advantage before you make any life-changing commitments. Give yourself this advantage with each offer you receive.

DAY

29

Negotiating, Accepting, or Declining an Offer

When offered a position, you have a series of decisions to make. You have already seen the need to consider whether this is a realistic commitment for you to make. Next you must determine what salary you will accept for this position. The employer must determine what salary the company is willing to pay for your services.

In order to make the necessary decisions about salary and accepting or declining a position, you should have already gathered information regarding a typical salary range for the kind of position you are seeking, for someone of your background and ability, in the geographic area where you are being offered the position.

▲

Know when to accept a salary offer and when to negotiate.

If you are staying in the same field in a similar position, you might expect to receive an offer 10 to 15 percent higher than your last position. If you are changing fields or geographic areas, you may be expected to accept less in salary based on the particular circumstances for your industry and area. If the industry has been cutting back on salary levels, you need to have this information before heading into salary negotiations with false expectations. Do your homework. If you know the going range for salaries in your field at this time, in this geographic area, you should be able to negotiate an agreement acceptable to both yourself and the employer. Following are some tips for negotiating salary once an offer has been made.

1. Try to have the employer start the negotiating with a salary range the company is willing to consider. This keeps you from starting too low or too high and pricing yourself out of a job offer.
2. If you are asked your salary requirements, respond by reiterating your understanding of the requirements of the position, the level of responsibility, and the way your duties would affect the profitability of the company. Then state the range of salary

you would expect, based on the industry information you have already gathered. Aim for the high
end of the range. Then ask if this is a range the
organization could entertain.

3. If you are not entirely pleased with the salary
   offered, ask for forty-eight hours to consider your
   decision. This will sometimes encourage the employer to offer an increase if he can do so.

4. Negotiate your next pay raise. Ask for a salary
   review in six months, within which time you will
   have opportunity to demonstrate your value to the
   employer.

5. Be careful not to ask too little. Many people who
   have been out of work for some time are willing
   to accept considerably less pay than they were
   making previously. This can work against you by
   making you appear desperate. Employers are also
   leery of losing employees who may be willing to
   accept a lower salary as a temporary measure,
   then continue the job search while using this position as a stopgap measure. Don't volunteer that
   you are willing to work for considerably less. If
   you are willing to take a substantial drop in pay,
   be able to show other benefits the job provides
   that makes this reasonable (such as not needing
   to commute as far, pay for monthly parking, and
   so on).

6. If the salary offer is firm, see if you can negotiate
   better hours, benefits, or working conditions that
   would make the salary worthwhile to you.

7. When discussing the salary you hope for, refer to
   factual information about salaries in the industry.

You might say something like, "I have done a little research, and my understanding is that this position typically pays something in the range of _____ within the industry. Is my information correct?"

8. If you will not be able to live with the salary/benefit offer presented, thank the employer sincerely but express your regrets.

Personal Evaluation

- Do you know the actual salary range being offered for the type of position you are seeking, in the industry you are considering, for someone of your background and ability, in the pertinent geographic area?
- Are you willing to try negotiating for the best salary offer you can get?

Action

1. Practice negotiating salary with someone. Rehearse your lines based on actual information you have gathered regarding salaries for the kind of position you are seeking.
2. Tape your practice negotiations so that you can review the tape and make necessary improvements.

Encouragement

Many people feel uncomfortable discussing money. By preparing and practicing for this part of your job search, you will become more comfortable with the discussion. Gaining factual knowledge will help you know when to accept an offer and when you can reasonably negotiate.

DAY
30

Keeping the Job
You Find

If you have followed these steps to finding a job that is well suited to your abilities and interests, you should not have difficulty keeping the job you find. If you enjoy your work, feel comfortable with the salary/benefits package, and are fully committed to doing an excellent job, you should be able to adjust to your new position well.

The first sixty days of your new job are crucial. During this time the employer will be watching your performance closely, and you will be trying the job on for size. If you can make it through your first sixty days without being overwhelmed, you should feel good about yourself and the job. Continue to look for ways to use your abilities for the benefit of the company.

Every new relationship requires a period of adjustment. You can expect to feel somewhat uncomfortable until you find your way around and build relationships with your co-workers. Don't worry about being a bit nervous at first. Just focus your attention on fulfilling the promises you made while interviewing for the position.

------------------▲------------------

The first sixty days of your new job are the most important.

Motivational speaker Zig Ziglar observes, "Some people stop looking for work as soon as they find a job." Be sure that this saying is not true of you. Do your best every day to benefit the employer for whom you work and to help the company achieve its goals. Look for new ways to use your abilities, and develop yourself in ways that are personally satisfying and professionally productive where you are now. When you do a great job where you are, you can't help but move up in the world.

Personal Evaluation

- Once you find a job or now that you have found a job, are you willing to keep the promises you made during your interviews?
- Could anyone rightfully describe you as someone

who stops looking for work once you have found a job?

Action

1. Keep the promises you made to the interviewer before you accepted the job. Your self-confidence will be enhanced, and your employer will be glad she chose you.
2. Continue to look for ways to benefit the company, further convincing your employer of your value.

Encouragement

When you do a great job within a company that is well suited to your interests and abilities, you create the best insurance possible against having to seek a job again anytime soon.

Food for Thought

A hundred times every day, I remind myself that my inner and outer life are based on the labors of other men, living and dead, and that I must exert myself in order to give in the same measure as I have received.

—Albert Einstein

Bibliography

1. Blatner, Howard. *Acting-In. Practical Applications of Psychodramatic Methods.* New York: Springer, 1973.

2. Fagan, Joen, and Shepherd, Irma, eds. *Gestalt Therapy Now.* Palo Alto, California: Science and Behavior Books, 1970.

3. Moreno, J. L. *Psychodrama*, Vol. I. Beacon, New York: Beacon House, 1946 (revised 1964).

4. Moreno, J. L. *Psychodrama: Action Therapy and Principles of Practice*, Vol. 3. Beacon, New York: Beacon House, 1969.

5. Perls, Frederick S. *Gestalt Therapy Verbatim.* Lafayette, California: Real People Press, 1969.

6. Perls, Frederick S., Hefferline, Ralph, and Goodman, Paul. *Gestalt Therapy.* New York: Brunner Mazel, 1973.

7. Perls, Fritz. *The Gestalt Approach and Eyewitness to Therapy.* Palo Alto, California: Science and Behavior Books, 1973.

8. Rolfe, Bari. *Behind the Mask.* Persona Products, 1977.

9. Spolin, Viola. *Improvisations for the Theater.* Evanston, Illinois: Northwestern University Press, 1963. An excellent source of warm-ups.

DATE DUE

DATE DUE			
MAR 1 2 1996			
MAR 1 3 1996			
FEB 0 4 1997			
JAN 1 7 1997			
			Printed in USA